T0293275

Reputations at Stake

Reputations at Stake

WILLIAM S. HARVEY

OXFORD
UNIVERSITY PRESS

Great Clarendon Street, Oxford, OX2 6DP,
United Kingdom

Oxford University Press is a department of the University of Oxford.
It furthers the University's objective of excellence in research, scholarship,
and education by publishing worldwide. Oxford is a registered trade mark of
Oxford University Press in the UK and in certain other countries

Published in the United States of America by Oxford University Press
198 Madison Avenue, New York, NY 10016, United States of America

British Library Cataloguing in Publication Data

Data available

Library of Congress Control Number: 2022948739

ISBN 978-0-19-288652-1

DOI: 10.1093/oso/9780192886521.001.0001

Printed and bound in
the UK by Clays Ltd, Elcograf S.p.A.

Contents

Acknowledgements   x

1. Reputation Matters   1
   Diagram 1.1: The Rewards and Risks that Reputation
     Brings to Organizations   2
   Reputation Forms at Many Levels   5
       Individual Level   5
       Team Level   6
       Organization Level   6
       Regional Level   7
       Country Level   8
       Phenomena Level   9
       Environment   10
       Social Movements   11
       Health   12
       Technology   12
   Diagram 1.2: The Multiple Levels of Reputation   13

2. Reputation: What It Means and Where It's Made   14
   What Is Reputation?   14
   Table 2.1: Theories and Perspectives of Reputation   16
       Reputation and Its Fragility   16
   Table 2.2: Unpacking My Definition of Reputation   17
   How Multiple Reputations Impact our Lives   18

3. Reputation and Power: How Reputation Is Built,
   Maintained, and Subject to Threat   20
   How Did You Decide Who to Vote For?   20
   Who Are the Electorate Voting For?   23
   Stakeholder Capitalism and Stakeholder Theory   25
   Diagram 3.1: An Inside-Out Approach to Stakeholders   28
   Diagram 3.2: An Outside-In Approach to Stakeholders   28
   Existential Threats   29
   Intermediaries   31

Diagram 3.3: Past and Present Comparisons of
Information, Media Stories, and Reputations 32
Diagram 3.4: The Causes, Realities, and Outcomes of
Reputation 33

4. How Migration Affects the Reputations of
Countries and Cities 36
Reputation of Places 37
Diagram 4.1: Multiple Reputations that Inform
Migration Choices 39
Intermediaries Connecting Skilled Migrants With
Countries 39
Labour Market Reputation 40
Return Migration and Brain Circulation 42
Diagram 4.2: The Importance of Reputation for
Home and Host Countries 44

5. The Global Scale of Reputation and Crisis
Management Across Multiple Borders 46
Multiple Reputations Across Borders 47
Diagram 5.1: The Multiple Reputations of PromCon 48
Social Media Reputations: The Dark Side 49
Social Influencers and the Spotlight They Shine on
Reputations 51
Cross-border Crises 53

6. Maintaining Positive Reputations Amid
Corruption and Competing Stakeholders 58
Navigating Corruption and the Needs of Competing
Stakeholders: Lessons from Econet in Zimbabwe
and Alacrity in India 58
Diagram 6.1: Four Types of Stakeholder Positions to
Ethical Behaviour 60
Navigating the Needs of Competing Stakeholders:
Lessons from Rio Tinto in Madagascar 62
Navigating the Needs of Competing Stakeholders:
Lessons from Libraries Unlimited 64
Diagram 6.2: Location of Fifty-four Libraries of
Libraries Unlimited 65
Diagram 6.3: Libraries Unlimited Stakeholders 66

Table 6.1: Libraries Unlimited Mission and Six Core
    Purposes   67
Table 6.2: Terminology when Formulating a Strategy
    at Libraries Unlimited   68
Diagram 6.4: Five Core Objectives   69
Table 6.3: Stakeholder Quotations   70
    A Summary of Navigating Competing Stakeholders   71

7. Aligning Purpose and Values   73
Diagram 7.1: Misalignment of Society, Purpose, and
    Values   74
Purpose   74
Diagram 7.2: Excerpt From the Business Roundtable's
    (2019) Statement on the Purpose of a Corporation   75
Business Action on Purpose   76
Diagram 7.3: Five Examples of Business Action on
    Purpose   77
Organizational Values and How They Can Be
    Internalized Within Organizations   81
    Creating Values in HKL   81
Diagram 7.4: Alignment of Purpose, Values, and
    Identities   82
Diagram 7.5: Internalizing Values Through Leaders,
    Managers, and Employees   83

8. Responding to Threats   86
Reputation and Identity Conflict in Management
    Consulting   88
Table 8.1: Types of Identity-reputation Gaps and
    Responses   89
Diagram 8.1: Reducing the Gap Between Identity
    Claims and Reputation   90
Leadership and Cultural Change in Meat Processing   91

9. Doing Well by Doing Good   96
Surfwell: Health and Wellbeing Within Devon and
    Cornwall Police   97
Diagram 9.1: Surfwell   97
    How Does Doing Good Make an Organization Do
        Well?   98
Pivoting During a Global Financial Crisis in Executive
    Recruitment   100

Diagram 9.2: Managing Reputation in Response to
Common Threats 104
The Konyaks of Nagaland: Compassion Among
Headhunters 104
Diagram 9.3: Balancing Toughness and Kindness 106
Daoist Nothingness: SME Leaders in China 107

10. The Growing Threat of Professional Misconduct 112
Background on the Prison Project 113
What Causes People to Commit Professional
Misconduct? 115
Diagram 10.1: Individual Triggers of Professional
Misconduct 116
Individual Triggers 117
Organizational Context 120
Diagram 10.2: Organizational Context Drivers of
Professional Misconduct 122
Environmental Milieu 122
Diagram 10.3: Environmental Milieu Drivers of
Professional Misconduct 124
Diagram 10.4: Professional Misconduct: An Outcome
of the Layering of Individual, Organizational, and
Environmental Factors 124
Layering of Individual, Organizational, and
Environmental Factors 124

11. Recovering From Reputation Damage 126
How Inmates Are Planning their Recovery 128
Diagram 11.1: Three Overlapping Phases of Recovery 128
Phase 1: Despondency and Loss of Identity 129
Phase 2: Acceptance, Self-Realization, and
Transition 129
Phase 3: Thinking and Planning Recovery 130
The Way You Fall Affects How You Climb 131
Diagram 11.2: How Process, Prominence, and
Proximity can Improve or Worsen Recovery From
Reputation Loss 134
Contribution Is the Most Important Anchor to Climb 134
What Can We Learn From Inmates About Recovering
From Reputation Damage 136

12. Concluding Remarks   138
    Recap   138
    Reputations at Stake   141
    What Can We Do? Some Cautionary
        Recommendations   144
    Diagram 12.1: Cautionary Recommendations   148

References   149
Index   163

Acknowledgements

I would like to thank Claire Hilton for helping me to sharpen the structure, storyline, and narrative of the book. I am grateful for the financial support from the University of Exeter Business School to develop the book. I would also like to thank the team at Oxford University Press for helping me to improve the book's wider appeal. I dedicate this to my parents, brother, wife, and two children who are the rocks in my life and who have been unwavering in their love and support to me.

1

Reputation Matters

Does reputation impact what you do? As children, how we perform in exams or interact with our peers affects how others perceive us. As adults, our success at applying for jobs or promotions is impacted by evaluations and judgements that others make of us. What we wear and own, what we say, who we interact with, where we work, what clubs we belong to, what we do with our time, and how we present ourselves in the real and virtual world all influence the perceptions that others have of us. Some people also reflect on and talk about their legacy, indicating that reputation can remain important long after death.

Years of research have revealed how reputation is formed, its importance and its fragility. On these pages, through a range of global examples across many sectors, you will come to understand why reputation matters, what threatens reputation, and what steps can be taken to mitigate reputation damage.

Reputation is not only something that we need to think about as individuals, but also in relation to our organizations, whether we are leaders, managers, or employees. I hear you say: 'Why should I care about reputation when I am not responsible for or paid to worry about such strategic issues?' My answer is that as an employee your collective actions and behaviours have an impact on the perceptions of the quality of the product or service that you are delivering. If this is perceived as excellent, then your organization will have a strong platform from which it can be financially sound and meet the needs of different stakeholders. It will also increase the likelihood of repeat purchases, further investment, and other good employees wanting to work for your organization. An ambivalence or disinterest in your organization's reputation means you are unlikely to influence the direction of your organization. Therefore you will gain limited meaning from your work, which will affect

Reputations at Stake. William S. Harvey, Oxford University Press. © William S. Harvey (2023).
DOI: 10.1093/oso/9780192886521.003.0001

how others perceive you and your organization, and this could undermine its financial performance and the engagement and satisfaction of a wide group of stakeholders. At best, this might lower performance and morale within your organization; at worst it could undermine its sustenance and lead to you and your colleagues being laid off. Reputation is at stake for all of us because it swings both ways, bringing both risks and rewards.

Let us begin by looking at reputation as a valuable intangible currency that allows organizations to accrue many rewards (Rindova et al., 2010) (see Diagram 1.1).

Diagram 1.1 The Rewards and Risks that Reputation Brings to Organizations

Reputation allows organizations to accrue rewards in five main ways:

1. Higher Pricing. Organizations with positive reputations can charge higher prices for their products and services. Think, for example, of what Apple Inc. charges its customers for an iPhone compared to other smartphone providers; or what McKinsey & Company bills its clients compared to other management consulting firms.

2. Public Recognition. Organizations with positive reputations start to gain public recognition, for example in mass and social media. The Global RepTrak® 100 provides a reputation ranking for the world's leading companies, which in 2021 rated the LEGO Group as number one, followed by Rolex and Ferrari. These are all prominent organizations who tend to receive significant public attention.

3. Attracting and Retaining Talent. Those who have positive reputations can both attract and retain talent, which provides them with a strategic advantage in the labour market compared to their competitors. There are many notable media organizations that provide such rankings: *Fortune's 100 Best Companies to Work For* rated Cisco, Salesforce, and Hilton as the three top companies in 2021. Such rankings inform how different stakeholders perceive organizations, as well as decisions around applying for and remaining with employers.

4. Expanding into Allied Fields. Once organizations have built an established reputation for something, it enables them to expand into allied fields. It is worth reflecting on how Amazon.com, Inc. started out in 1994 as an online bookseller and has subsequently expanded into a multi-billion-dollar multinational technology firm focusing on e-commerce, cloud computing, digital streaming, and artificial intelligence.

5. Attracting Investment. Organizations with positive reputations can attract investment from a variety of sources such as venture capitalists and shareholders, helping them to grow.

But reputation also has a downside and presents major risks for organizations too. There are six major risks associated with negative reputations:

1. Disengaged Customers and Clients. A negative reputation can disengage customers and clients. In 1991, Gerald Ratner, the CEO of a British jewellery company, gave a speech at the Royal Albert Hall in London, in which he jokingly said that its products could be sold at such a low price 'because it's total crap'. Following the speech, £500 million was knocked off the firm's value and it very nearly collapsed. This lack of consideration for the customer gave rise to the expression 'doing a Ratner'.

2. Assumptions of Poor Quality. Negative reputations lead to assumptions of poor quality. A low average rating on Booking.com, for example, will negatively impact on the perceptions of the hotel among customers, which in turn will inform their purchasing decisions.

3. Unwanted Attention. Negative reputations bring unwanted attention in the mass media, social media, and in face-to-face networks. Consider, for example, all the negative media attention that Prince Andrew's sexual assault lawsuit brought to the British Royal Family.

4. Demotivation of Employees. Negative reputations demotivate employees and affect the ability for organizations to attract new and retain existing employees. Not surprisingly, potential and existing employees do not want an organization's negative reputation having a contagion effect on their identities (who we are) and their own reputations (what do others think of us) (Brown et al., 2006).

5. Difficulties attracting investment. Poor reputations create difficulties for attracting investment, whether that is a founder starting a business or a leader seeking to expand a business.

6. Poor Performance. Negative reputations lead to poor performance, as BP plc found with the Gulf of Mexico oil spill and the Volkswagen Group found in light of its emission scandal. In some

cases, such as Enron, a sustained or extreme negative reputation event (e.g. large accounting fraud) can lead to the demise of an organization.

Reputation Forms at Many Levels

Reputations are formed and held at various levels.

Individual Level

At the individual level reputation has an impact on how we are perceived within business and society. When we write a cover letter for a job, share our CV, or write on LinkedIn, this is about trying to create an intended image: what we want others to think about us. But this is not the same as reputation, which is what others *actually* think of us (Brown et al., 2006). Therefore, employers will use additional methods to form an impression of job candidates, including word of mouth, references, and assessments. Reputation continues to be important for us within organizations because how we are perceived by managers will impact on how we are appraised and therefore our salary, promotion potential, and wider esteem within the organization.

The reputation stakes are often even higher for founders and leaders when they are considered the figurehead of the organization, meaning that different stakeholders within and outside of the organization pay careful attention to their actions and behaviours. Elon Musk, the Founder and CEO of Tesla, for example, gains major attention across mass and social media when he makes any public statements, which not only impacts on his own reputation but also on the reputation of Tesla itself. The actor Will Smith captured unwanted attention at the 94th Academy Awards in 2022 when he stormed the stage and slapped comedian Chris Rock for making an offensive joke about Smith's wife. Minutes later Smith was walking onto the same stage to receive the award for Best Actor for his performance in *King Richard*, which was a jarring contrast from his earlier outburst.

Reputation is also highly relevant for individuals within society. This is a double-edge sword, as individuals can be held in high-esteem in villages, towns, and cities for their contributions to the community, but can also find themselves stigmatized and socially ostracized if they are perceived negatively. Walking this knife edge is not only something that we as adults need to be mindful of—it is also vital to educate our children about it, particularly given how perceptions are formed in person as well as online, for example through social media, gaming, and the metaverse where the boundaries between virtual and reality become blurred. Our actions online can be long-lasting, and may inform how others perceive us many years later.

While some might shun the idea of caring about one's reputation and letting it affect their life choices (particularly when happiness might be at stake), whether we like it or not it is important for us to consider because it has a ripple effect on what we do and where we go.

Team Level

Reputations are also formed in teams. Within large investment banks, law firms, or management consultancies, although the organization may have prominent reputations (e.g. JP Morgan, Baker McKenzie, or McKinsey and Company), it can also be the department or team that attracts talent. This is as true in financial and professional services as it is in sports, music, and film. For example, while the reputation of the New England Patriots, an Andrew Lloyd Webber West End show, or a Stephen Spielberg production will be highly important in influencing perceptions among different groups, the team and their reputation is essential for influencing the organization's reputation as well as the reputation of individuals, whether that is a chair, CEO, sports coach, composer, or film director.

Organization Level

Organizational reputation is a well-established field of literature (Fombrun, 1996; Roberts and Dowling, 2002; Rindova et al., 2005; Lange et al., 2011; Ravasi et al., 2018; Bustos, 2021) and there are a wealth of reputation rankings for organizations (e.g. *Fortune's* Most Admired Companies, The *Times Higher Education* World Reputation Rankings and *Vault's* Best Companies to Work For). As I discussed earlier, there are rewards for positive reputations but risks of reputation damage, which is why it is a strategic imperative that needs careful oversight and management by board members and executives. The Deepwater Horizon explosion and oil spill in the Gulf of Mexico in 2010, for example, led to eleven deaths and the largest marine oil spill to date. This event rapidly escalated into a major reputation disaster for BP; it led to federal criminal charges of manslaughter, the replacing of the CEO, around $65 billion in costs, charges, and penalties, and it took many years for the company's share price to recover.

Organizations can also impact their reputation through social advocacy. Ben and Jerry's long-term advocacy of lesbian, gay, bisexual, transgender, and queer (LGBTQ+) justice issues through social media has been perceived as a good fit between its identity and the issues that it has been advocating (Lim and Young, 2021). This has had a positive impact on Ben and Jerry's reputation; however it would have had a different outcome for their reputation had the company been seen as opportunistic rather than authentic in its advocacy. Conceptually, we should distinguish between advocacy related to promoting social issues when organizations are authentically expressing their views and acting on issues such as diversity and inclusion or climate change, and advocacy related to promoting the business when organizations are leveraging their customers or procuring intermediaries such as influencers to extend their brand awareness. These two forms of advocacy can sometimes be conflated when organizations seek to promote social or environmental causes owing to business opportunism rather than because such actions align to their purpose.

Regional Level

Regional reputation arises when cities or places influence the choices of different stakeholders, for example as a travel destination for tourists, an environment for investors, or a location to live for employees. Saxenian (2007), for example, referred to the important draw of Silicon Valley as a region for aspiring engineers in the information and communications technology sector, which has been argued elsewhere in the contexts of financial services in Singapore (Beaverstock, 2002), scientists in Boston (Harvey, 2011a), and tourism in Dubai (Dutt and Ninov, 2016), to name only a few examples. Michael Porter (2000) has highlighted the importance of location for competitive advantage, and Richard Florida's (2005) work on the creative class (from engineers, scientists, and designers to entrepreneurs, lawyers, and programmers) argues that talent plays an essential role in economies, regions, workplaces, and societies. How places create the right infrastructure, services, and environment to attract and retain talent has major implications for the subsequent success of the region. Hence the reputation of the destination, whether that is Silicon Valley or Shanghai, will have an impact on flows of talent (Harvey et al., 2018).

Country Level

The Economist's liveability survey of cities and HSBC's expat explorer survey of countries are just two of many prominent ranking systems that influence the reputation of places which impact on travel and relocation choices. This is not to mention the countless articles published in newspapers and magazines, or the even larger volume of television, film, and social media coverage of cities and countries that shape the reputation of places. Despite the costs, many cities are keen to host major events such as the Olympics or the FIFA World Cup because they draw significant attention to a city and country, which can inform trade, travel, investment, and mobility choices. However, the reputation of places is not always plain sailing. In 2022, for example, the UK and particularly London came under severe criticism during the Russia-Ukrainian war for being a place of money laundering. *The Economist* produced a short documentary on so called 'Londongrad', asking why it is so easy to hide dirty money in Britain (*The Economist*, 2022).

Phenomena Level

The final form of reputation is opaquer because it does not relate to any scale of analysis, but instead refers to an event or movement. Phenomena level reputation stems from important, remarkable, or unprecedented events, states, movements, or situations: it could relate to political events such as the geopolitical tensions and war between Russia and Ukraine, the heated US Presidential elections of 2020, or the narrow UK referendum vote to leave the European Union in 2016. It could also relate to an economic, environmental, health, or social phenomenon.

Phenomena level reputation has become particularly pressing in the last few years given the rise of 'stakeholder capitalism' (also referred to as stakeholderism)—a form of capitalism in which companies are not seduced by short-term profits for shareholders, but seek long-term value creation by considering the needs of all their stakeholders and society at large (Schwab and Vanham, 2021b). Economically, this has become a burgeoning discussion point in Western countries. In 2019, the Business Roundtable, an influential body that represents 181 of the largest companies in the United States, modified its guiding principle on the purpose of the corporation, shifting away from shareholder primacy, which was advocated by the likes of the American economist Milton Friedman and the former CEO of General Electric, Jack Welch, to a broader commitment to all its stakeholders. The British Academy (2018) has taken a similar position in its report 'Reforming Business for the 21st Century', which argues that the purpose of the corporation should come first before profit (see also Mayer, 2020).

Stakeholder capitalism is not merely an academic concept (Hill and Jones, 1992; Freeman et al., 2010) with limited practical relevance, or a business fad with no legitimate evidence base (Schwab and Vanham, 2021b). There are countless branches of this phenomenon that show how the reputation of stakeholder capitalism is gaining legitimacy among different groups, from corporate social responsibility (Smith, 2003), the triple bottom line (Elkington, 1997), Certified B Corporations (B Corporation, 2021), the United Nations' 17 Sustainable Development Goals

(UN, 2021), sustainable finance (Schoenmaker and Schramade, 2019), and the circular economy movement (Ellen MacArthur Foundation, 2021) to name only a few examples.

Environment

Many of the examples that relate to stakeholder capitalism connect with the environment, which is another phenomenon that divides perceptions. Think, for example, of the tensions between the enormous body of scientific data around the human impact of climate change, and groups and organizations who reject climate change. Often such groups communicate and engage within echo chambers, which creates division around climate change among the wider population. The UN's annual Conference of the Parties (COP) has led to increasing political consensus at a global level around communications and emissions commitments since the first COP meeting in Berlin in 1995. However, the reputation of environmental phenomena such as climate change, biodiversity depletion, air, and water quality are perceived very differently among various groups, often depending on their vested interests, economic status, political power, and geographic location. Unfortunately, those who are most severely impacted around the world (i.e. the poorest) often are the most limited in their ability to instigate changes in perception because of their lack of voice. The Extinction Rebellion is an example of a global environmental movement that attempts to challenge this by subjecting themselves to significant reputation damage through their civil disobedience in the pursuit of pushing governments to avoid climate tipping points (Lenton et al., 2019).

What is concerning is that our impact on the environment is already extending into space up to and beyond 100 miles above the earth's surface, which is the lowest altitude at which satellites can maintain orbits for a reasonable time. The National Aeronautics and Space Administration (NASA) estimates that there are more than 27,000 pieces of space junk. This orbital debris is tracked by the Department of Defense's global Space Surveillance Network sensors (NASA, 2021). This excludes a much larger volume of debris that is too small to be tracked. It is estimated that there are around 900,000 pieces between 1 and 10 centimetres in length and potentially 128 million pieces that are at least 1 millimetre in length (*The Economist*, 2021c). Travelling at around 15,700 mph in low orbits, much of this orbital debris could cause major damage to human and robotic spacecrafts. This is another example of tension between the demands of governments, organizations, and people to have fast internet and the wider impact this has on the environment. In the words of Jonathan McDowell, an astrophysicist at the Harvard-Smithsonian Center for Astrophysics (*The Economist*, 2021c: np):

> Every time humanity moves into a new domain—the oceans or the air or space—we go, 'Wow, this is enormous and really empty, we can throw as much garbage here as we want, and it'll never fill up, right?' Then pretty soon we go, 'Oops, that wasn't quite true.' And we're reaching that point in space.

Social Movements

Social examples of reputations that relate to phenomena are also highly prevalent. The #MeToo movement was a social campaign against sexual abuse and sexual harassment, with the purpose of empowering, through empathy and solidarity, people who have been sexually assaulted. The Black Lives Matter movement focused on advocating against police violence towards Black people. The Occupy Wall Street movement protested economic inequality and began in the financial district of Wall Street in New York City. These are all examples of the mobility of social groups around issues that were considered pressing for societies. The reputation of such phenomena among a wider set of stakeholders is important for determining their momentum. Connecting with wider groups helps to increase attention, improve the flow of resources, and provide a stronger mandate for change, whereas alienating stakeholders can undermine the legitimacy of a movement and the ability to instigate change.

Health

There are also health examples of how reputations relate to phenomena. For example, there were different perceptions within and between countries around the seriousness of the 2020–2022 coronavirus pandemic. Even when there was strong consensus—due to the number of deaths and the high volume of hospital admissions—that COVID-19 was a virus that required serious attention by everyone, many governments have since been criticized for their complacency. Within those countries in the privileged position to vaccinate, there has generally been a strong uptake by populations. But there have also been large segments of the population, including prominent individuals such as the Serbian professional and world number one ranked tennis player Novak Djokovic, who have been sceptical about vaccines, despite compelling scientific data. Hence, the reputation of phenomena such as COVID-19 impacts on the policies and behaviours of different groups, which in turn influences outcomes such as positive cases, hospital admissions, and deaths.

Technology

Finally, there are technological illustrations of the reputations of phenomena. The volatility around the value and application of cryptocurrencies, for example, has divided opinion among investor winners and losers. Other examples include how technology firms use data for commercial purposes and who should own the data, or how technological firms who operate across multiple geographic locations should pay tax. A further example concerns the uncertain future of the metaverse and how humans interact with and present themselves, which literally blurs the boundary between the real and virtual worlds, with uncertain reputation consequences.

These examples illustrate how reputation does not necessarily reside in a country, region, organization, or individual, but within the phenomenon. This reputation is important because it influences new policy, the emergence of markets, and shifts in behaviour.

In summary, reputation envelops everything that we do and operates at multiple levels (see Diagram 1.2), from people and entities to locations and phenomena. Now that we have identified the rewards, risks, and multiple levels of reputation, let's clarify what reputation means and how it impacts us.

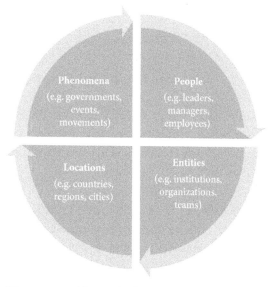

Diagram 1.2 The Multiple Levels of Reputation

2

Reputation

What It Means and Where It's Made

What Is Reputation?

Now that the risks and rewards of reputation have been set out, let us
look to what is meant by reputation and how it impacts our daily lives.
Reputation has been defined and framed in many ways by many people.[1]
I define reputation as:

> The multiple perceptions of an entity made by different stakehold-
> ers, based on their evaluations of the past capabilities and character
> of the entity, and their assessment of its ability to provide future
> contributions.

How I have come to define it in this way is a result of the work of many
others in this field. Fombrun (1996, 2012), for example, has argued that
there are three important attributes of reputation: collective assessment;
specific to a set of stakeholders; relative to a reference group. Walker
(2010) extended these attributes further, suggesting that reputation can
be positive or negative, and stable and enduring.

It is broadly agreed that reputation is a collective evaluation of an
entity, which could range from a country, organization, team, or individual. That evaluation stems from a group of stakeholders (Dowling, 2016)
who are forming perceptions based on past activities and expectations
around future behaviour (Harvey et al., 2020).

---

[1] (Fombrun, 1996, 2012; Gotsi and Wilson, 2001; Wartick, 2002; Walker, 2010; Dowling,
2016; Ravasi et al., 2018, Pollock et al., 2019). Definitions of reputation have been extensively
detailed by Barnett et al. (2006) and have also been discussed in relation to other forms of social
evaluations such as legitimacy, status, and stigma (Roulet, 2020).

Reputations at Stake. William S. Harvey, Oxford University Press. © William S. Harvey (2023).
DOI: 10.1093/oso/9780192886521.003.0002

Capability and character have also been documented as key aspects of reputation (Mishina et al., 2012; Waller and Younger, 2017; Park and Rogan, 2019). While capability reputations focus on quality and performance (which could include, for example, the financial performance of an investment bank), character reputations focus on incentive structures and behavioural tendencies (such as cases of professional misconduct) (Mishina et al., 2012: 460).

Reputation has been defined from multiple theoretical perspectives, including institutional theory, agenda-setting theory, stakeholder theory, signalling and impression theory, identity theory, resource-based theory, and social construction theory (Fombrun, 2012: 96). I do not detail them here because these have been covered extensively and it is not the focus of this book, but I do provide more details in the footnote for those of you who would like more information. An alternative way to understand reputation is through seven theories and six perspectives, presented by Fombrun (2012)[2] and Ravasi et al. (2018) respectively,[3] in Table 2.1.

---

[2] Institutional theory focuses on the wider context and environment in which reputation develops. Agenda-setting theory suggests that the media plays a powerful role in shaping public perceptions of organizations. Stakeholder theory focuses on different groups who hold a stake in the actions and outcomes of organizations. Signalling and impression theory highlights how organizations seek to influence the impressions of and support from different groups to support their interests. Identity theory focuses on how people within the organization define it. Resource-based theory refers to the key resources that organizations require to be competitive within their sector and recognizes that different groups co-construct shared understandings of organizations, which include identifying and legitimizing rankings and ratings that highlight winners and losers.

[3] The game-theoretic perspective focuses on how reputation influences competitive interactions such as expectations around future behaviours, and on how reputation can be formed by signals sent by actors. The strategic perspective builds on signalling theory, recognizing reputation as an intangible asset that can be valuable for its interactions with different stakeholders. The macro-cognitive perspective highlights the importance of information exchanged and influenced by different actors, including intermediaries, which contribute to both prominence and favourability (Rindova et al., 2005; Lange et al., 2011). The macro-cognitive perspective suggests that reputation is socially constructed, with social media playing a particularly important role (Etter et al., 2019). The micro-cognitive perspective emphasizes how individuals access and process information in order to make judgements about organizations. This literature recognizes that reputation is multidimensional and based on information being processed at an individual level (Bitektine, 2011; Lange et al., 2011; Harvey et al., 2017b) even if this is based on short cuts and crude proxies. The cultural-sociological perspective suggests that a wider group of public actors inform reputation, including politicians, artists, business media, and, more recently, social media influencers. Ravasi et al. (2018: 580) distinguish between *reputation entrepreneurs* (e.g. journalists or public relations experts) who have a stake in giving a particular position on organizations, compared to *reputation arbiters*, who position themselves as providing a seemingly objective assessment of organizations (e.g. rankings). The communicative perspective stems from corporate communications where organizations would seek to

Table 2.1 Theories and Perspectives of Reputation

Seven ways of theorizing reputation: 96–98)	Six perspectives of reputation (Ravasi et al., 2018: 575–582)
Institutional Theory	Game-Theoretic
Agenda-Setting Theory	Strategic
Stakeholder Theory	Macro-Cognitive
Signalling and Impression Theory	Micro-Cognitive
Identity Theory	Cultural-Sociological
Resource-Based Theory	Communicative
Social Construction Theory	

My definition of reputation builds on this literature and my own previous definition of organizational reputation (Harvey, 2021a). To help clarify my definition, I summarize some of its key terms in Table 2.2.

Reputation and Its Fragility

A central premise of this book, highlighted in the title, is that reputations are at stake everywhere. I use the term 'at stake' for two purposes. First, to show the risk reputation can present. At the time of writing, the 27-year-old international England cricket player Ollie Robinson was suspended by the England and Wales Cricket Board for offensive tweets he made a decade ago as a teenager, leading to an intervention by the UK Prime Minister, Boris Johnson. This demonstrates how past actions, even from years ago, can undermine one's reputation. A few months later, a major scandal hit English cricket with Pakistan-born Azeem Rafiq breaking down in tears in front of UK members of Parliament as he outlined the racism, bullying, and inhumane treatment he faced while playing cricket for Yorkshire that impacted on his career and almost led to him taking his own life. Here the example shows that the experience of an individual can significantly impact the reputation of a club, a community, an organization, and a sport practised all around the globe.

project the organization in particular ways to external stakeholders. This has broadened to how organizations engage with different groups through various forms of communication processes to shape their reputations over time.

Table 2.2 Unpacking My Definition of Reputation

Key Terms	Explanation
Multiple perceptions	Recognizes that reputation is based on perceptions rather than facts and that stakeholders vary in what they think.
Entity	While much of the reputation literature has focused on organizations, I use the term 'entity' to capture the broader ways that reputations exist for phenomena, industries, institutions, organizations and individuals.
Different stakeholders	Reputation is not a reflection of one person or group's perceptions, but the multiple perceptions within and between different stakeholder groups.
Evaluations	Reputation is not an impulsive or fleeting impression, but a considered judgement of an entity.
Past capability	Stakeholders often make evaluations based on the quality and performance of institutions, organizations, and individuals in the past.
Past character	Stakeholders make judgements of the ethical and moral tendencies of entities based on their past actions and behaviours.
Future contributions	Stakeholders assess what are the likely future outcomes from an entity.

My Definition:

The multiple perceptions of an entity made by different stakeholders, based on their evaluations of the past capabilities and character of the entity, and their assessment of its ability to provide future contributions.

The second reason I use the term 'at stake' is to show that reputation is inextricably linked to its stakeholders. As my definition implies, there is no single reputation, but often multiple and sometimes even conflicting reputations depending on the stakeholder in question. As I have argued elsewhere (Harvey, 2021b), prominent organizations such as Apple Inc. can have markedly different reputations depending on the stakeholder group. Its strong sales of iPhones and thirteen-fold growth in its share price has meant it has had a strong reputation among customers and investors. Environmental stakeholders, however, would direct our attention to the firm's environmental footprint in the production, running, and disposal of its products. Even within a stakeholder group, there may be divided opinions: governments, for example, would welcome the jobs and economic growth that Apple brings to national and regional economies, but would likely take issue with the company's approach to competition, data privacy, and tax contributions. Hence, a major challenge with reputation is that it varies depending on the stakeholder group. But even this is a simplistic representation of reputation, because within stakeholder groups there can be marked variation. There is no one homogeneous view among the US democratic party, employees of Green Peace, or shareholders of Google. Reputation not only varies within and between stakeholder groups, but also cuts across multiple scales of analysis, meaning that it is hard to ignore.

How Multiple Reputations Impact our Lives

The concept of reputation has been defined in many ways because it cuts across multiple academic fields and theories, and because it is relevant to governments, organizations, and individuals. Reputations are at stake for us all because of the rapid potential upside and downside. In their book *Brand Vandals*, Earl and Waddington (2013) argue that thanks to the internet and social media, organizations do not own the conversation around their products and services. They are also limited in their ability to monitor and observe how multiple audiences engage with them. Nevertheless, they do need to engage with reputation management because circumstances can change rapidly. Note how fast individuals and businesses with limited reputation can become household names in politics, business, music, film, sport, and environmental activism. For example, Emmanuel Macron's launching of *En Marche* propelled him to a two-term presidency of France. Note also how easily those who are in the public spotlight can fall from grace. For instance, the contrast of Nobel Peace Prize winner Aung San Suu Kyi leading her National League for Democracy to victory in Myanmar's first openly contested elections in twenty-five years in 2015, but then being removed and arrested by a military coup in 2021. Ironically, although reputations can rise and fall quickly, for those of us who are forming impressions of others, reputation can be sticky and difficult to shift.

One of the major challenges for any organization or individual seeking to maintain and enhance their reputation is ensuring their purpose is both aligned to shifting societal expectations and to their internal values. In the subsequent chapters you will see the big picture challenges of reputation for countries, governments, regions, and cities; the considerations that organizations face in navigating multiple competing stakeholder demands; and the rapidity of reputation downturns for individuals.

The last part of the book focuses on the importance of reputation for individuals, and draws on a unique research project of seventy inmates who have committed professional misconduct in the United States. To help us understand how to rebuild reputation, we look at the root causes of reputation damage and what can we learn from this group. In the final chapter you will find a summary of why reputations are at stake, and some recommendations building on theory, case studies, and examples.

Let us begin with the bigger picture, where reputation impacts governments, events, and movements.

3

Reputation and Power

How Reputation Is Built, Maintained, and Subject to Threat

How do government officials get into positions of power within liberal democracies? By securing the necessary number of votes. But how do individuals decide who to vote for? And who are the electorate voting for? Different forms of reputation play an important role in answering both questions.

How Did You Decide Who to Vote For?

Ultimately, when making a choice of who to vote for, we are guided by many perceptions we hold. There are numerous stakeholders who can influence our choice, and our social networks have a strong influence on how we think about others. The foundational work of American sociologist Mark Granovetter (1973) distinguished between our strong and weak ties. Simplistically, strong ties are family members, friends, and close colleagues with whom we have close social interaction, whereas weak ties are the acquaintances and associates from different spheres of our lives who are less well known to us. Both sets of contacts can have an impact on our access to information and influence our percep-tions. Family and friends can strongly influence our choices, and this can be shaped from a young age and reinforced over time. The princi-ple of homophily argues that people hold ties with others with similar social characteristics to themselves (McPherson et al., 2001). As a result, our networks—whether family, friendship, work, or community—are homogenous in terms of the kinds of people we interact with and

Reputations at Stake. William S. Harvey, Oxford University Press. © William S. Harvey (2023).
DOI: 10.1093/oso/9780192886521.003.0003

their personal characteristics, perceptions, and behaviours. Now is the time to wonder how homogenous your own networks are. This idea of homogenous networks is also apparent among people who hold extreme views. Political psychology research, for example, shows that people with more extreme and more conservative views tend to be more homophilious in their networks than people with more liberal and moderate views (Boutyline and Willer, 2017).

Another important stakeholder that influences our perceptions is traditional mass media. This includes television, newspapers, magazines, and radio where there is a one-way process of creating information for many consumers (Livesey, 2011). This media takes a position on political parties and their leaders. *The New York Times*, for example, endorsed President Joe Biden in the 2020 United States elections, whereas *The New York Post* endorsed President Donald Trump. Similarly, Fox News supported Donald Trump and the Republican Party, whereas CNN advocated for Joe Biden and the Democratic Party. Because people tend to read the same newspaper or watch the same news programme, or because their newsfeed settings on their electronic devices show similar kinds of stories, this will influence the kind of content they read, watch, or listen to, thus informing their voting choices.

Since the rise of social media platforms, a blurred boundary has emerged between our family, friends, colleagues, and acquaintances (social networks) and the news, magazines, television, and radio content we consume (mass media). This is the new mass media (which includes websites, computer games, and, of course, social media platforms). It involves peer networks and two-way communication between many participants who act as both producers and consumers of information (Livesey, 2011).

It is well known that people's choices around political parties tend towards partisanship, despite the opportunity for accessing online and offline sources that provide perspectives that are different to their prior beliefs (Guess et al., 2021). Because we can choose who to follow on social media platforms, our choices inform the algorithm that determines what content we see. The impact of this has us consuming stories that affirm and reaffirm our prior beliefs about governments, organizations, and people. This runs the risk of creating a fixed mindset that can make reputation sticky and hard to shift. It adds to the existing challenge that people tend to listen to and watch the same channels, buy the same newspapers and magazines, and speak to people in familiar professional and social circles. Hence, perhaps we should not be surprised when we read about the splintering or polarizing of societies.

The proliferation of social media platforms, from Facebook and YouTube to WeChat and TikTok, provide a forum for 3.78 billion and counting social media users (Statista, 2021) to interact socially and share content. Because of the sheer number of users, coupled with the role of advertised content and social media influencers, social media is becoming a powerful force that is influencing how people perceive political leaders and parties. Social media is also accelerating the speed of influence. For example, on Thursday 24 June 2021, the UK Secretary of State for Health and Social Care, Matt Hancock, was seen having an affair with a former lobbyist, Gina Coladangelo. By the following day, the Prime Minister had accepted Hancock's resignation, and by Saturday 26 June a new Secretary of State for Health and Social Care, Sajid Javid, had been appointed. This event shows how the confluence of social networks, mass media, and social media can influence the speed and impact of political events today.

Reputation is as important in democracies (ruled by many) as it is in oligarchies (ruled by a few) and autocracies (ruled by one). In June 2021, the Chinese Communist Party celebrated its 100th year anniversary. Within the Chinese context, *guanxi* refers to informal connections between people which are maintained through mutual commitment, loyalty, and obligation (Chen and Chen, 2004). *Xing* is trust, which is considered vital for enhancing the quality of *guanxi*. Because *guanxi* is underpinned by three broad groups (families; classmates, colleagues, or neighbours; strangers), reputation is important because it reflects how people are perceived by these different groups. This has a strong impact on their family, community, and labour market opportunities. China's President Xi Jinping, a chemical engineering graduate from the prestigious Tsinghua University, is considered a 'princeling'—a child of elite senior officials—and he is married to the famous contemporary folk singer Peng Liyuan. In different ways, these various networks have been important for helping him to build his reputation among different groups.

We know from the work of French sociologist Pierre Bourdieu that elite networks and connections in school structures have a powerful influence on the political career outcomes of those individuals in France. Stephen Taylor at the University of Exeter has found a similar trend with university education in the UK, with a very large proportion of cabinet and shadow cabinet ministers in the last fifty years being educated at either Cambridge or Oxford. As Taylor and others observe (see Maclean et al., 2017), this is not only a trend we see in political leadership, but also in the upper echelons of charities, journalism, media, and business. In other words, who we are connected with and how we are connected to others within different social structures impacts on our access to key people and information. While the mere connection to another person may be described as part of a social network, this should not be confused with social capital, which is the resources that can be exchanged through network ties (Lin, 2001). This influences the reputations of people across different networks (Glückler and Armbrüster, 2003) and therefore their political career outcomes. However, while an individual's reputation is important, are political supporters voting for the individual or something else?

Who Are the Electorate Voting For?

When people cast their vote or express their endorsement, it is not clear who they are voting for. We often assume that it is an individual because they represent the face of a movement, a political party, a conference, an election, or a media campaign. Indeed, there is a strong association between how leaders are perceived and how the organizations they serve are perceived. Hayward et al. (2004) find that journalists over-attribute the actions and outcomes of organizations to their CEOs, rather than wider situational factors, which can lead to over-confidence and hubris among leaders. This is likely to extend to political leaders who receive a lot of coverage from journalists; an article might lead to glowing celebrity status when there is fair sailing, or infamy when the waters are rough. Lovelace and colleagues (2021) use the term 'CEO celebrity' to describe leaders of organizations who attain a celebrity status, which, if the wrong context exists, can lead to unfavourable outcomes for the organization. While this study's focus is on CEOs, there is an important link to other contexts such as political leaders who are inevitably highly prominent in terms of coverage in the media. When things are going well, this works in favour of the leaders and their political parties, but when there are difficulties then it causes greater attention on both groups.

Third parties such as the media can develop characters for dramas, from organizations such as a political party, a corporation, or a firm. This can enable celebrity or infamy outcomes for these organizations (Zavyalova et al., 2017). Often these outcomes can be divisive because reports can be mixed: they are reaching different audiences, which is creating fragmentation in the public domain, including on social media platforms (Roulet and Clemente, 2018). Although the focus is on how new mass media and other third parties focus on celebrity organizations, this is also true of celebrity leaders (Lovelace et al., 2021). While the literature on celebrity leaders has focused on business leaders and in particular CEOs, as I mentioned above politicians and other leaders inevitably attract major scrutiny from the media and other third parties to help create narratives and drama. Reflect, for example, on the mass and social media coverage of former President Donald John Trump before, during, and after his election as the 45th President of the United States. Graffin and colleagues (2013) show in their research on the 2009 Members of Parliament (MP) annual expense scandal in the UK that while high status political leaders were not more likely to abuse the expense system than their low status MP counterparts, they were more likely to be targeted by both the press and voters for the inappropriateness of their expenses claims—something I discuss later in the book when covering reputation loss. Status and prominence can increase the risk of what the authors refer to as 'falls from grace and the hazards of high status'. Importantly, this is not only about receiving negative news, but typically escalates further in terms of those elite individuals remaining in post. In short, mass and social media are doing more than just presenting news; they are influencing wider perceptions among the public and influencing decision-making.

When the public are voting for political leaders, they are influenced by many groups: the leaders themselves (e.g. the Labour Party candidate for Prime Minister), the political party (e.g. the Conservative Party), the local representative (e.g. the MP candidate for the Liberal Democrats), newspapers (e.g. *The Guardian*), television (e.g. Sky News), magazines (e.g. *The Economist*), followers on social media platforms (e.g. Twitter), and many others, including those within family, friendship, and work networks. This raises the importance of understanding how reputations form through stakeholder groups.

Stakeholder Capitalism and Stakeholder Theory

As I discussed earlier, there has been a proliferation of references to stakeholder capitalism in the last few years.[1] This has been in the wake of references made by influential business and academic groups.[2] One of the earliest business advocates was Klaus Schwab, Executive Chairman of the World Economic Forum who has written about the concept and phenomenon of *Stakeholder Capitalism* (Schwab and Vanham, 2021b). The authors claim that at the heart of the stakeholder model are people and the planet. They suggest that people and planet are central, alongside four other stakeholders who have their own set of primary objectives:

1. Companies who focus on profits and long-term value creation;
2. Civil society's focus on each organization's purpose and mission;
3. Government's pursuit of equitable prosperity;
4. The international community's focus towards peace (Schwab and Vanham, 2021b: 179).

Schwab and Vanham emphasize the symbiotic relationship of these groups, as over time one cannot succeed without the other. For example, a highly profitable business that has large carbon dioxide emissions, produces significant landfill, and erodes biodiversity brings into stark

---

[1] Examples include material from well-known business publications such as *The Economist*, Harvard Business Review, and McKinsey Quarterly
[2] Examples include the Business Roundtable, the British Academy, and the World Economic Forum.

tension the relationship between people and planet. Equally, note corporations that shirk their responsibilities to contribute fairly to tax or who do not embed themselves within the communities where they operate undermine the purpose of the corporation, which should be: 'to produce profitable solutions to the problems of people and planet, and not to profit from producing problems for people or planet' (Mayer, 2020: np).

One of the reasons for the acceleration towards stakeholder capitalism is the recognition that the *modus operandi* for business is not sustainable in the long-term. Global political instability, unprecedented levels of inequality (Piketty, 2014), biodiversity depletion, and a climate emergency are just a few existential threats suggesting that the current political and economic model is not working for either the people or the planet.

Alongside what we have witnessed in business and society, there have been long-standing intellectual debates around agency theory[3] and stakeholder theory.[4] Bower and Paine (2017) make a persuasive argument in *Harvard Business Review* that the agency-based model of maximizing shareholder value as the primary goal is deeply flawed. They argue that the notion that shareholders own the corporation is both legally confused and raises questions around accountability, not to mention the wider ethical and moral responsibilities of companies to people and planet. The authors cite both governance and management practices that have increased the power and influence of particular shareholders, without establishing their wider responsibilities and accountability.

Despite the predominance of agency theory in the last few decades, there has been a steady shift towards stakeholder theory and the acknowledgement of the contractual relationship that organizations of

---

[3] Agency theory dates to the 1970s when information economists referred to the agency relationship between one party (the principal) who delegates work to another party (the agent). This concept is examined in detail by Eisenhardt (1989a) and explains the challenges of cooperative effort within business and society (Ross, 1973; Jensen and Meckling, 1976). This whole body of work has focused on the relationship between leaders and shareholders (Hill and Jones, 1992).

[4] Stakeholder theory argues that for any business to be successful it must create value for customers, suppliers, employees, communities and financiers, shareholders, banks, and other people with the money. It says that you cannot look at any one of their stakes or stakeholders, if you like, in isolation. Their interests must go together, and the job of a manager or entrepreneur is to work out how the interests of customers, suppliers, communities, employees, and financiers go in the same direction.

all structures have to a wide set of stakeholders such as employees, customers, suppliers, creditors, communities, and the wider public (Hill and Jones, 1992). Each organization, whether it is national or local government, a corporation, a partnership, or a start-up, will have its own set of stakeholders who provide the organization with a resource, which they expect in exchange that their interests are satisfied (March and Simon, 1958). Voters and tax payers, for example, provide the organization (i.e. government) with their vote and a proportion of their income, and in return they expect the government to fulfil its pre-election commitments and to offer good value for money for their contribution. Other examples that I have argued elsewhere (Harvey, 2021b) include shareholders giving organizations capital through buying shares and in return they expect a favourable return on their investment over a particular time horizon. Alternatively, employees provide organizations with their time, skills, and expertise, and in return they expect a fair wage, good working conditions, and positive career prospects. Hence, organizations need to carefully consider their exchange relationship with multiple groups, which is the essence behind stakeholder theory.

It is one thing recognizing the value of different stakeholders (Donaldson and Preston, 1995), but another to establish how to meaningfully engage with them. The influential work of Ronald Mitchell and colleagues (Mitchell et al., 1997) argues that managers of organizations want to achieve goals, which is driven by their purpose. Within this frame of reference, they will form perceptions that will determine the importance of different stakeholders. These perceptions will determine how they identify different classes of stakeholders based on three attributes: the perceived *power*, *legitimacy*, and *urgency* of the stakeholder. Using a Venn diagram to represent these three attributes, the authors create a typology of stakeholders for managers of organizations to consider as important. This valuable inside-out perspective is informative for helping organizations to understand who their key stakeholders are and how they might engage with them (see Diagram 3.1).

An alternative approach to stakeholder engagement is an outside-in perspective (see Diagram 3.2). This approach focuses on how an organization can be important for different stakeholders so that the latter can support the purpose of the organization. This argument is not about the stakeholders who are considered important by leaders

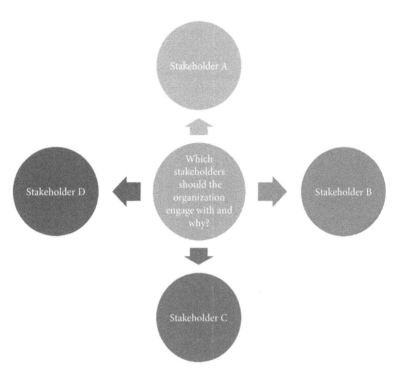

Diagram 3.1 An Inside-Out Approach to Stakeholders

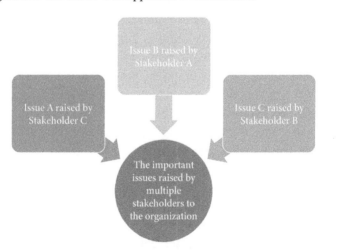

Diagram 3.2 An Outside-In Approach to Stakeholders

and managers of the organization, but understanding what the issues are that these different stakeholders consider important (McVea and Freeman, 2005). Of course, it is possible that there may be tensions between stakeholders who approve or disapprove of the favourable or unfavourable treatment of other stakeholders (Lange et al., 2020). This also helps to develop strategy because organizations move beyond what might seem obvious and trite (for example that the electorate are important for political parties, or employees are valuable for professional service firms), to specific issues that have hitherto been unknown to the organization such as that the electorate want urgent policy and investment action on biodiversity depletion or that employees value autonomy more than salary bonuses in the workplace. This is not to suggest that leaders can necessarily always address these issues—although in many cases they can but their resistance to change (Kegan and Lahey, 2009) blocks them from doing so. However, an outside-in approach can provide leaders with valuable data to inform their strategies, policies, and communications.

Existential Threats

Governments and all organizations often find themselves having to pivot into new areas in response to external criticism or threats. This is challenging because the legitimacy of a government can be compromised if it is accused of a U-turn in policy. There are few clearer examples of this than how national governments have approached, fared, and been perceived around their handling of the coronavirus pandemic. One day a government is perceived as taking the right approach to lockdowns, the next it is considered too slow at opening up the economy, or too slow in its administration of rolling out a vaccine programme. I have no desire to weigh in on the relative strengths and weaknesses of how different governments have performed, but what is clear is they have had to swiftly shift their approach in response to new data and stakeholder perceptions. Hampel and colleagues (2020) have argued how new ventures find themselves having to pivot their business because their original approach failed, and this is also true of new and established governments who introduce new policies. This can create tension between those stakeholders who supported the policy and those who rejected the policy, which can create existential threats for organizations (Hampel et al., 2020).

It is tempting to conclude that the coronavirus pandemic is an outlier that threatens a government's reputation. However, there are many examples of major events that can shift how a government is perceived. Ukrainian President Zelensky's approval rating surged in February 2022 to more than 90% among Ukrainians, compared to 31% in the December before the Russian invasion (Fitri, 2022). Ten days following the 9/11 terrorist attacks in New York in 2001, for example, President George W. Bush's declaration of a war on terror contributed to the highest presidential job approval rating (90%) ever measured in six decades by Gallup (Gallup, 2001). The massacre of fifty-one people at two mosques in Christchurch in 2019 was one of the worst terrorist attacks in New Zealand's history. The Prime Minister, Jacinda Ardern, received very strong support for her public compassion and empathy towards the Muslim community and for wearing a headscarf when she met with the families of the victims, showing her sensitivity to the cultural context. The following year she was voted into office for a second term after a landslide victory for her handling of several crises.

Not only governments but all kinds of organizations can face major threats to their existence. Think about BP's Deepwater Horizon oil spill crisis in 2010, Volkswagen's emissions scandal in 2015, the Duke and Duchess of Sussex's interview with Oprah Winfrey criticizing the British Royal Family in 2021, or Mark Rutte's government submitting their resignation to the King of the Netherlands in 2021 following thousands of parents being falsely accused of child benefits fraud. These examples show that governments, corporations, royal families, and other organizations can face existential threats. Indeed, many leaders and organizations experience reputation setbacks and failures every day. Often the ones we watch, read, or hear about are those that involve prominent individuals and organizations. The above examples are existential threats around either the capability of the organization, such as its financial performance or operations, or its character, such as its ethical code of conduct or values (Mishina et al., 2012; Waller and Younger, 2017). Another form of threat faced by governments are common threats which are those that are not particular to any one individual or organization, but common to a sector, multiple sectors, or wider societies (Harvey et al., 2019). Examples include global recessions, pandemics, climate emergencies, world wars, and major terrorist or cyber attacks. Governments play a central role in navigating these threats, and how they frame and communicate their actions have important implications on how they are perceived by different groups.

Intermediaries

How we perceive political leaders and the organizations that they represent is also determined by intermediaries. Intermediaries are third parties such as popular, mass, and social media. They could include coverage within television news channels such as CNN, newspapers such as *Le Monde*, radio stations such as the BBC, magazines such as *The Economist*, internet sites such as Apple News, and social media platforms such as WeChat. The variety and scale of reach of intermediaries is vast. When you combine this reach with prominent individuals who have an extensive following across multiple platforms and media channels, then it becomes apparent how important they are in informing public opinion on people, organizations, and issues. As I have argued elsewhere (Harvey, 2021a), most industries have social media influencers who work across multiple platforms such as YouTube. Some of them have many millions of followers and therefore what they say and do impacts on the perceptions of others. For example, with the crucial Georgia Senate runoff during the US 2020 election, Destiny, a professional gamer and political commentator, led one of the largest door campaigns of the election (Citarella, 2021). He managed to encourage his followers to knock on between 17,500 to 20,000 doors in Columbus, Georgia. This highlights how social media influencers, particularly for younger generations of voters, are a powerful force of influence. As the example illustrates, intermediaries are not neutral in their position on politics, business, or social issues. As I discussed earlier, mass media, whether that is television, radio, or internet news channels, also plays a powerful role in influencing the reputation of governments among large audiences (Deephouse, 2000) through the editorial position they place on themes and how they present news stories. This is evident, for example, in the different positions with which the media responded to Prince Harry and Meghan Markle's interview with Oprah Winfrey about the British Royal Family.

While different mass media has always segmented itself in relation to how it responds to political events, the landscape has significantly changed in the last decade. Michael Etter and colleagues (2019) argue that in the past there were common and fewer sources of news information where media organizations would present relatively similar stories, albeit with a different editorial or political stance, which would cause relatively homogeneous impressions among different audiences. In contrast, today's media landscape has multiple institutions, individuals, and media organizations creating content, which is shared, refracted, and repackaged on multiple social media platforms, creating highly heterogeneous and often polarizing impressions from different audiences (see Diagram 3.3).

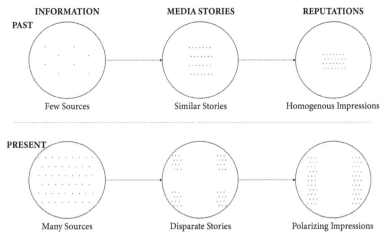

Diagram 3.3 Past and Present Comparisons of Information, Media Stories, and Reputations

Diagram 3.4 The Causes, Realities, and Outcomes of Reputation

Reputation is important for all forms of organization, including governments. Leaders and managers need to understand how reputations are formed because they impact on their actions and behaviours, and influence how they are perceived and perform. One way of articulating the importance of reputation is by considering its causes, realities, and outcomes (see Diagram 3.4).

The cause of a particular reputation is affected by past actions. Organizations do not operate within a vacuum; they are compared to a set of competitors. Think Apple and Microsoft, PwC and Deloitte, or Boeing and Airbus. The same is true of governments (e.g. the Conservative and Liberal Parties in Canada, and the BJP, INC, and JD in India). Organizations need to be mindful that their past actions can impact their ability to affect change in the future. Reputation is 'sticky' and not easily changed over time because different stakeholders, from employees to clients and investors, do not readily accept such change (Schultz et al., 2001). Many stakeholders have past experiences with organizations that colour their perceptions: they recall an unfulfilled manifesto pledge or a service that was delivered to them, or they remember how a member of an organization treated them. There are, then, a proliferation of intermediaries, including but not limited to mass and social media, who shape what we think about organizations.

The reality of a reputation is multi-layered, informed by different causes and often with conflicting perceptions (Harvey, 2021a; Harvey et al., 2017b). For example, a government could have a positive reputation for its approach to one policy issue (e.g. climate change), but a negative reputation for its approach to another policy issue (e.g. reducing inequality). The reputation of organizations can also vary between stakeholders. For instance, they might have a positive reputation among investors, but a negative reputation among regulators. Alternatively, a national government or organization operating within a global environment might have a positive reputation in one country or region, but a negative reputation in another place. Finally, it is obvious that reputation is not static but can change over time, and that how organizations are perceived over time can vary.

One of the reasons why reputation is so important is because of its outcomes. A government with a positive reputation is going to increase its chances to secure votes; a charity that holds a positive reputation for representing good causes is likely to receive significant donations; a company that has a positive reputation for its products and services is likely to receive repeat custom over time. Organizations who hold positive reputations benefit from both attracting and retaining high quality workers. They also have greater flexibility in terms of pricing and expanding into new allied markets. While the examples above describe the outcomes of a positive reputation, there are clearly undesirable consequences for negative or ambivalent reputations, which is why regular consideration of reputation is a valuable investment of time for all organizations, including governments. Finally, the outcomes of reputation are significant because they also have a circular influence on the causes of reputation in the future.

This chapter has primarily looked at the power of reputation for governments. A government's reputation impacts on voter behaviour, but it is more complex because there are multiple reputations at stake: the reputation of the political leader, the party, the manifesto they put forward, the issues they advocate for, and how they are presented by different groups such as mass and social media. The different issues and the many groups that require consideration lie at the heart of the stakeholder capitalism movement where leaders of governments and other organizations need to be aware of and address the expectations of a wider set of stakeholders. One disparate group who have an enormous impact on countries, regions, and cities is migrants. Throughout human existence, people have moved and have had a major impact on economies and society. As I will show in the next chapter, how they perceive different places will influence their mobility choices, which will then impact on the reputation and competitiveness of different places.

4

How Migration Affects the Reputations of Countries and Cities

When we decide where we want to travel on holiday, we are likely to be informed by many sources such as videos, photos, reviews of places online, and discussions with travel agents, family members, friends, and colleagues. Or maybe we have been influenced by the location of a film, travel documentary, or radio programme. This is also true of people in desperate need who have been forcibly displaced because of persecution, war, poverty, or climate change. They also target particular countries, cities, and regions to move to. Although the levels of need are polar opposites, where holidaymakers and refugees choose to migrate are both likely to be informed by many reputations. If reputation influences our choices as tourists (think of all those reviews you have looked at online before booking a trip) then it is likely to be as important, if not more so, when we are making longer-term decisions such as forced and voluntary migration choices. Throughout 2021, there were tensions between France and the UK because of the flow of 26,000 migrants, mostly asylum seekers, on small boats between Northern France and the south of England. One of the reasons for this large and precarious flow of migration, which has led to countless deaths and rescues in the English Channel, is that many asylum seekers have existing networks in and perceptions of the UK that is driving their desire to move there. The same has been the case for the 2022 war between Russia and Ukraine, during which many Ukrainian refugees have wanted to move to the UK but have not been able to because of UK government visa restrictions and processing problems.

Reputations at Stake. William S. Harvey, Oxford University Press. © William S. Harvey (2023).
DOI: 10.1093/oso/9780192886521.003.0004

Reputation of Places

While I was interviewing highly skilled British and Indian scientists working in the world-class pharmaceutical and biotechnology sector around Boston, USA (Harvey, 2011a), I asked them why they moved from their home countries. Some interviewees referred to gaining their 'BTA'. I had heard of an MBA (Master of Business Administration) and an MPA (Master of Public Administration), but what was a BTA? The answer was 'Been To America', meaning gaining experience of working in the US was an important reputation-related rubber stamp on their CVs that would signal the quality of their credentials. Similar trends have been found on the west coast of the United States in Silicon Valley, which has attracted a large flow of highly skilled foreign engineers over many decades. AnnaLee Saxenian (2007) refers to a historical joke among technologists in Silicon Valley that its success was built on 'ICs': rather than 'Integrated Circuits', the term refers to the influx of 'Indian and Chinese' talent. This is by no means a US phenomenon, with Jon Beaverstock (2002) showing that foreign talent has gravitated to global cities with strong reputations such as Singapore and that there are many other examples of where foreign talent is attracted by the reputations of cities, from Vancouver to Hong Kong, Singapore to Dubai, Paris to Bangalore, and Shanghai to Sydney.

As is well known from our historical understanding of social networks (MacDonald and MacDonald, 1964), once people experience living in a particular place this is then shared among their social networks; this in turn informs the perceptions of others, and when positive will influence future flows of migration. While social network theories of migration are well established, the proliferation of sharing information through the internet and via social media and instant messaging means that the reputations of places can be built and destroyed at unprecedented speeds. What is noticeable is how a larger pool of individuals can more easily create and share content, for example through mobile devices, social media platforms, and instant messaging groups, to inform perceptions of places. My colleague Dimitria Groutsis and I (Harvey and Groutsis, 2015) found that not only do the reputations of origin and destination countries influence the migration choices of whether people stay in their existing country or move to another, but these people are also important producers of reputations in these countries through their direct experiences and through the information they share via social networks, which informs impressions among wider pools of people.

One way of understanding how reputation influences migration is through the concept of destination reputations. This is when multiple reputations impact on migration choices such as country, city or region reputation, organizational reputation, and other reputations that are important for prospective migrants (Harvey et al., 2018). I refer here to reputations in the plural because people do not make decisions based on one but many reputation criteria. For example, a potential Vice President employee of Meta from India will likely be interested in the reputation of the United States (country), San Francisco (city), Meta (company), and Mark Zuckerberg (CEO). A large and growing number of reputation rankings might help to inform that person on their choice such as country reputation (e.g. HSBC expat explorer survey), city reputation (e.g. *The Economist*'s liveability survey), organizational reputation (e.g. Fortune's most admired companies), and CEO reputation (e.g. Forbes' CEO awards). Of course, these are just a few of many reputation sources that may (or may not) inform this person's migration choice.

It is not only that multiple reputations inform migration choices (see Diagram 4.1), but that individuals may place different levels of importance on various factors (Velamuri et al., 2017a), meaning that sometimes these are likely to conflict with each other (Harvey, 2021a). Returning to the above example of the Indian Vice President of Facebook candidate, she may be excited about working for Facebook and the CEO, Mark Zuckerberg, but less enthralled about relocating her family to the San Francisco Bay Area and the related business, education, and cultural upheaval of living and working in the US. This simplification of the multiple and conflicting reputations that influence migration choices mean that people will focus on factors that are most salient to them. As discussed in the previous chapter in the context of mass and social media, another important factor that informs perceptions and decision-making is the role of intermediaries.

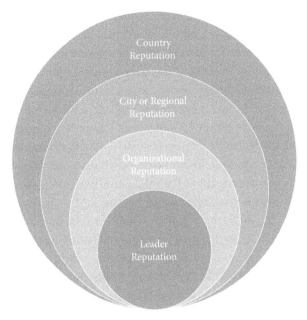

Diagram 4.1 Multiple Reputations that Inform
Migration Choices

Intermediaries Connecting Skilled Migrants
With Countries

Intermediaries of skilled migrants are individuals and groups who use
social networks to connect skilled migrants in their country of origin
with information, services, and social contacts related to labour market opportunities and integration resources in the country of destination
(Groutsis et al., 2015; van den Broek et al., 2016; Harvey et al., 2018).

It is well known from the migration literature how intermediaries
play a powerful role in influencing decisions. Most of the literature has
focused on illegal transactions carried out by intermediaries such as
human traffickers and people smugglers as well as legitimate bodies such
as government agencies and charitable organizations enabling desperate
and vulnerable people to migrate (Salt and Stein, 1997; Brown and Scribner, 2014). Intermediaries also play a powerful and invisible role in the
movement of skilled migrants.

It is striking to learn of the breadth of intermediaries, from recruitment agents and executive search firms to government agencies, migration and rankings agents, and online and offline forums committed to relocating skilled migrants. In many cases, skilled migrants are not influenced by one but multiple intermediaries. Imagine, for example, a Nintendo gaming executive in Kyoto headhunted by executive search firm Egon Zehnder to a C-Suite role in EA Vancouver. This person has professional contacts who work in the gaming industry and live around Vancouver, has seen that the city ranks highly in Mercer's quality of living survey, and is persuaded by conversations with the partner of the executive search firm as well as with a migration agent who can advise about neighbourhoods, schools, and other relocation considerations. In short, there are a proliferation of intermediaries for skilled migrants who shape the perceptions of the country, city, and organization, which, alongside other intermediaries discussed in the previous chapter, will influence perceptions and decision-making around whether this executive will stay in Kyoto or move to Vancouver.

Labour Market Reputation

Reputation of place is often affected by labour market reputation. Building on research with Tim Morris (Harvey and Morris, 2012), I define labour market reputation as *the reputation of organizations among potential and existing employees.* Labour markets are where workers (labour supply) compete with one another for paid employment, while employers search for work (labour demand). As I discussed above with the two potential employees of Meta and EA, labour markets can vary from being global in scope to more national and local in orientation.

The 'war for talent' argument introduced by McKinsey & Company (Chambers et al., 1998; Michaels et al., 2001; Guthridge et al., 2008) suggests that organizations need to give increasing focus to attracting and retaining their best workers. The argument is that the competition for talent is growing, and that organizations need to attract and retain employees to remain competitive and to bolster their labour

market reputations. However, this is not without criticism, including from Malcolm Gladwell, who referred to the Talent Myth within
Enron:

> They were there looking for people who had the talent to think outside
> the box. It never occurred to them that, if everyone had to think outside
> the box, maybe it was the box that needed fixing.
>
> (Gladwell, 2002: 33)

Despite some scepticism around organizations over-emphasizing talent,
a positive reputation of an organization among employees is important for both morale and productivity within the workplace (Gray and
Balmer, 1998). Evidence also suggests that employee expectations of
their organizations are growing (Pruzan, 2001) because the reputation
of their organization has implications for their individual identities and
sense of self-worth.

Reputation surveys of companies also emphasize the importance of
labour market reputation. *Vault*'s Best Companies to Work For and *The
Times*' Top 100 Graduate Employers, for example, annually provide
potential employees with information on organizations. Surveys such
as these, alongside discussions within a person's social networks, will
inform a decision to apply for and accept a job. In a study of 430 students
at the University of Oxford (74% undergraduates and 26% postgradu-
ates), for example, the reputation of an organization was something that
students considered quite carefully and that came into their reasoning
when applying for jobs (Harvey, 2011b). Former employees also impact
labour market reputation in positive and negative ways because they can
act as assets or liabilities for their former organization, which can spill
over into how other stakeholders perceive the organization (Hayward
et al., 2004). Contrast, for example, the impact of a former employee who
has started a successful business versus a whistle-blower opening the lid
on the toxic work culture of their former employer. Hence, labour market reputations are important for organizations to manage because they
impact on the attraction and retention of their talent pools, which are an
important source of their competitive advantage.

While reputation is valuable for all organizations, Charles Fombrun (1996) argues that it is particularly significant for organizations that provide services:

> Questions of reputation are of particular concern to knowledge-based institutions like consulting firms, law firms, investment banks, hospitals, and universities; their most valuable assets—the services they provide—are largely intangible. Economists call the services of these groups 'credence goods'—goods that are bought on faith, that is to say, on reputation.
>
> (Fombrun, 1996: 7)

Ironically, while many professional and financial service firms have built elite reputations (the Big Four accounting firms such as PwC and Ernst and Young; the magic circle law firms such as Hogan Lovells and Norton Rose Fulbright; bulge bracket banks such as Goldman Sachs and JPMorgan Chase), and while this has helped attract talent from around the world, many of them have struggled marketing their organization (Harvey and Mitchell, 2015), which has consequently hampered their ability to enhance their global reputations in different markets.

Having established that labour market reputations influence flows of skilled migration, what happens once the skilled migrant has gained the experience they want? Do they return to their home country, or do they stay? Let us look at the powerful role reputation plays in relation to return migration and brain circulation.

Return Migration and Brain Circulation

Somewhat confusingly, 'return migration' and 'brain circulation', which describe different processes, have tended to be used interchangeably. Return migration describes people who have emigrated to another country and later decide to return to their home country. For example, the term 'Boomerang Poms' describes the very large number of British migrants who move to Australia and later return to the UK. This I have first-hand experience of, having emigrated from a postdoctoral fellowship at the University of Oxford to a Lectureship position at the University of Sydney, before returning to a Senior Lectureship position at the University of Exeter.

This idea of return migration or boomeranging is not the same as brain circulation, which is when skilled migrants move between a host country (the country a person has migrated to), home, and other countries for business, work, and investment purposes (Harvey, 2012). Often brain circulation follows the first wave of skilled migration. Saxenian (2007), for example, describes the educational, professional, and network advantages from which IT technicians and engineers benefitted when moving from countries like China and India to the United States. Despite criticism of the brain drain—where developing countries are concerned about the loss of their homegrown talent—Saxenian argues that these groups have a strategic advantage and are providing significant benefits to their home countries through working abroad:

> Silicon Valley's Taiwanese engineers, for example, have built a vibrant two-way bridge connecting them with Taiwan's technology community. Their Indian counterparts have become key middlemen linking U.S. businesses to low-cost software expertise in India. These cross-Pacific networks give skilled immigrants a big edge over mainstream competitors who often lack the language skills, cultural know-how, and contacts to build business relationships in Asia.
>
> (Saxenian, 2002: 2)

How does this relate to reputation? Dimitria Groutsis and I argue that the relative reputations of home and host countries have an impact on very large flows of skilled workers (Harvey and Groutsis, 2015). As indicated in Diagram 4.2, if a skilled migrant holds a positive impression of the host country relative to their perceptions of the home country then they are likely to stay (brain gain), whereas if they hold a positive impression of their home country compared to their host country then they are likely to either return and/or invest in their home country (brain circulation).

Reputation can also play a negative role in migration behaviour. For example, if an Israeli scientist is dissatisfied with her experience of living and working in France then this might cause her to return to Israel,

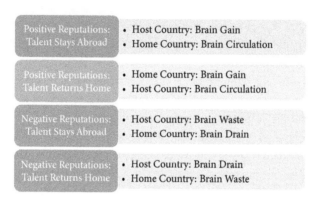

Diagram 4.2 The Importance of Reputation for Home and Host Countries

creating a brain drain in France because the country loses her talent, and a brain waste if she cannot find an appropriate job for her skills in Israel. Or if a nurse from the Philippines perceives that his skills are not valued in his home country compared to if he worked in Germany then this may encourage him to emigrate, creating a brain drain of nurses in the Philippines.

Although my description and diagram are a simplification of positive or negative reputations in what is a highly complex set of decisions, the wider point is that different forms of reputation, whether that is a home, host, or other country, a city or region, an organization or an individual, influences how people perceive places. This impacts on their migration and investment decisions. Hence, it is not surprising that some countries have invested in attracting talent. In 2008, for example, China introduced its Thousand Talent Program, which has attracted thousands of world-class Chinese scientists, entrepreneurs, and business workers living overseas to return to work in China. This kind of investment from the Chinese Communist Party sends a strong global message that it is keen to attract and retain the very best talent. It also contrasts with other national governments such as those of the US and the UK who have taken a more ambivalent approach to skilled migration in the last decade, even though both countries greatly benefit from foreign talent. Richard Florida (2005) argues that national and regional economies not only benefit economically from the presence of foreign talent, but there are also economic, social, and cultural benefits for cities, workplaces, and societies.

If we recognize that skilled migrants are important for the future of countries, then it is safe to assume that governments and organizations need to think carefully about how they manage their reputations across different international borders. This is especially the case when so much of what we do today—from consuming products and services to addressing political, health, and environmental challenges—requires communicating, cooperating, and working across borders. Reputations are challenged and held across the globe, so how can this be managed when people are operating across multiple borders and when they are having to respond to crises?

5

The Global Scale of Reputation and Crisis Management Across Multiple Borders

Our actions and behaviours have an impact on other people and places. Clicking 'Buy Now' on amazon.com has a whole string of implications for different international groups, including producers, suppliers, employees, custom officials, couriers, and others who are involved at different stages in the product's lifecycle. It is well known, for example, that responsible supply chain management (which includes social issues such as child labour, working conditions, and human rights as well as environmental issues, waste management recycling, and the use of natural resources) can enhance an organization's reputation (Hoejmose et al., 2014). Some organizations, such as Apple Inc. have complex supply chains that span multiple countries. These organizations need to be mindful that although responsible supply chain management can help to enhance their reputations, they can also damage them. In 2010, a series of suicides at Foxconn, the Taiwanese multinational electronics manufacturer in Shenzen, China, led to reputation damage and mounting media pressure on Apple Inc. because Foxconn was one of Apple's oldest and largest suppliers. This caused Apple to conduct its own internal review (as did Foxconn) and to make several changes in its labour practices. More broadly, this example shows the reputation damage that organizations can face from their supply chain. This is important because while in the past it may have been considered to be something that suppliers should manage, the onus is now on organizations to manage their reputation across their supply chain.

Reputations at Stake. William S. Harvey, Oxford University Press. © William S. Harvey (2023).
DOI: 10.1093/oso/9780192886521.003.0005

Multiple Reputations Across Borders

Organizations are increasingly responsible for managing their reputations through the actions and behaviours of their suppliers, and they also need to manage their reputations across international borders. It is important to recognize that many organizations, from McDonald's to Starbucks, VW to Rolex, and Hilton to Bosch, operate in multiple countries and therefore need to take into account the reputational risks as well as the opportunities of operating across different international borders. In March 2022, for example, Yale School of Management (2022) documented hundreds of global firms who had suspended their operations with Russia following its invasion of Ukraine. Some organizations such as McDonald's suggested that it was withdrawing from Russia altogether.

While I was researching the evolving reputation of a prominent global management consulting firm—let's call it PromCon to protect its identity—what was apparent was how many different and sometimes competing reputations it held. Using the metaphor of a prism, my coauthors and I suggest that often we are all operating under a false understanding of what reputation is: we believe it to be singular and often influenced by rankings, awards, and our own impressions, which tend to coalesce around a single lens (Harvey et al., 2017b). The reality is that organizations have multiple and competing reputations. In the case of PromCon, we found different layers of reputation. For example, we found that it had multiple reputations for something, with someone, and in someplace. We found that PromCon had a strong reputation for being pragmatic and was strong on restructuring, but relatively weak in entrepreneurship and strategy (something); its reputation was generally positive among clients and employees, although this was variable depending on the project and the level of the employee who was interviewed (someone); and there was a clear difference in the reputation of the firm internally and externally depending on the country (someplace). One Asian country, for example, was seen as the 'rising star', while a European country was considered as the firm's 'Achilles heel'. This example shows that a global professional service firm with the same brand, values, and leadership can have very different and sometimes conflicting reputations (see Diagram 5.1).

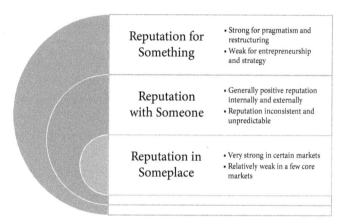

	Reputation for Something	• Strong for pragmatism and restructuring • Weak for entrepreneurship and strategy
	Reputation with Someone	• Generally positive reputation internally and externally • Reputation inconsistent and unpredictable
	Reputation in Someplace	• Very strong in certain markets • Relatively weak in a few core markets

Diagram 5.1 The Multiple Reputations of PromCon

To illustrate the wider point about the multiple reputations of organizations, consider the following examples. First, note how over the last decade Apple Inc. has had a generally very positive reputation among its customers for the quality of its products and among shareholders for its consistent financial performance, and yet it has received criticism from the media for its low tax contributions in different countries. Second, observe how customers of Sports Direct have generally been positive about the price of its products even if observers have questioned the firm's leadership and labour practices. Third, note how shareholders have generally been happy with the share price of Ryanair even if the media have latched onto the provocative comments of its CEO, Michael O'Leary. To give one example of his comments on passengers incurring a fee when they had forgotten to print their boarding passes: 'We think they should pay €60 for being so stupid'. I could continue with countless examples from around the world of where organizations have a positive reputation with some stakeholders but are strongly criticized by others, or where the organization has a divided reputation within a stakeholder group.

Managing the different expectations of shareholders comes back to stakeholder theory and stakeholder capitalism. Unfortunately, while many organizations are quite forthright in *saying* that they care about and engage with different stakeholders, there is less evidence that this is supported by what they are *doing*. For example, the term 'corporate social responsibility' (CSR) has been poorly defined and understood (Moir, 2001), and the business case for virtue has not been strong enough (Vogel, 2005). Porter and Kramer (2006) suggest that most corporate responses to CSR have been neither strategic nor operational, but cosmetic, with a focus on impression management through, for example, glossy CSR reports and persuasive imagery. Laufer (2003) goes further, arguing that there are parallels between social reporting and corporate compliance. A study of 100 acquisitions of public companies announced during the coronavirus pandemic found that despite the claims that corporate leaders would use their discretion to benefit the needs of different stakeholders, such claims did not seem to be supported by evidence, with shareholders and corporate leaders being the principal beneficiaries (Bebchuk et al., 2022).

Many organizations have been accused of either 'greenwashing' or 'bluewashing'. Seele (2017: 248) states that 'Greenwashing is a co-creation of an external accusation toward an organization with regard to presenting a misleading green message', whereas bluewashing derives from the United Nations, which is considered a moral authority on global values and governance and which uses the colour blue for its flag and logo. Hence, bluewashing is where organizations make misleading claims around human rights, including poverty eradication, disaster relief, and human rights (Seele, 2007). While there are many organizations who are strong on rhetoric and weak on action regarding their wider responsibilities to society, those whose actions really are a positive social force (a growing list) must convince a discerning audience fatigued by the slow pace of change. How are they to legitimize their reputations for responsible action amongst the prolific blue and greenwashing of established organizations? An arena in which this plays out in a very powerful way is social media.

Social Media Reputations: The Dark Side

As I discussed in Chapter 2, social media platforms have a powerful role in influencing perceptions of organizations and people. One of the most challenging aspects of reputation to come to terms with is that it does not necessarily represent fact or reality, but multiple perceptions. Therefore it requires careful management, without misleading or manipulative greenwashing or bluewashing. In fact, a preserving-one's-reputation-at-all-costs-through-an-obsession-with-impression management can have serious outcomes. For example, the 'Child Protection in Religious Organizations and Settings' report published by the Independent Inquiry Child Sexual Abuse (2021: np) found in England and Wales: 'egregious failings by a number of religious organizations, and cases of child sexual abuse perpetrated by their adherents'. In terms of reputation, what was particularly troubling in this report was the statement:

> In many cases, concerns about external involvement are connected to a desire to protect the reputation of a religious organisation.
> (Independent Inquiry Child Sexual Abuse, 2021: C8, 48–49)

In other words, despite the abhorrent nature of the acts, different people were unwilling to disclose what happened for fear of undermining the reputation of the religious organization or leader. This highlights the dark side of a relentless focus on reputation preservation.

Social media is a powerful intermediary that shapes how organizations are perceived among different groups. Increasingly, reputation is not only measured annually through an annual survey, which only provides a snapshot of reputation in time, but now can be monitored in real time and longitudinally through data mining social media platforms such as Twitter (Rust et al., 2021). The volume of people who use social media platforms and the speed with which information about organizations can be shared means that it is important that organizations are proactive in engaging with different audiences. An organization that was previously passive on social media and which then tries to respond to a crisis is likely to face scepticism among social media audiences. In contrast, an organization that has previously been proactively engaged with its audience and responds quickly and honestly to a crisis is more likely to receive the benefit of the doubt in the short term. Of course, there are also organizations who have been highly proactive on social media and have built up a lot of excitement among audiences only to catastrophically fail when the rhetoric is not matched by the reality. This is captured with the example of the Fyre Festival.

The Fyre Festival was the most talked about festival of 2017 and received major fanfare on mass and social media—but it ended in disaster. This was captured graphically in Netflix's 2019 documentary *Fyre: The Greatest Party That Never Happened*. The festival was billed as a glamorous and exclusive music festival on a deserted Bahamian island, where tickets cost up to $100,000 and guests were promised luxury accommodation and the best food, art, music, and adventure in the Bahamas. The event organizer, businessman Billy MacFarland, spared no expense in hiring filming and PR agencies, models, caterers, and social media influencers to build an intended image (what he wanted others to think about the festival) as the party of the year. Instead, what materialized was guests flying in and arriving at an incomplete building site, most promises being unfulfilled, the event being cancelled, and guests being stranded on the sparse island of Great Exuma and not being refunded. This was being captured in real time on social media and caused a subsequent media storm.

Following several indictments, in 2018 McFarland was sentenced to six years in a federal prison for mail and wire fraud. This case shows the high risk to reputation of overpromising and underdelivering. Although an extreme example, it highlights the severe reputation damage that misleading claims can cause for both organizations and individuals.

Social Influencers and the Spotlight They Shine on Reputations

Seth Crossno (known by the name William Needham Finley IV) is a blogger and podcaster who shared live pictures and videos of the Fyre Festival, which received millions of viewings and quickly influenced perceptions of the event. Such examples show the population reach of social media influencers. As individuals, social media influencers shape the perceptions and attitudes of audiences through the content that they produce and share (Freberg et al., 2011). Typically, these influencers are prominent and have high status, focus on specific topics in their posts, require engagement with and a following from large audiences, and are willing to monetize their activities (Abidin, 2015). Most interestingly, influencers produce, distribute, and interact with groups online, which provides them with the volume and quality of relationships to shape attitudes among wider groups (Enke and Borchers, 2019: 267). Hence, it is not surprising that many organizations are exploring how social media influencers can help and hinder their marketing, sales, and PR activities.

Daniel Wellington (DW), a watch company founded in 2011 by the Swedish businessman Filip Tysander, used social media influencers effectively to raise awareness among audiences. How? As DW priced its watches in the premium category (more expensive than common watches, but cheaper than luxury watches), it targeted 18- to 35-year-old Gen Ys from upper to middle incomes and focused on two steps (Krows Digital, 2020). First, it understood the importance of recognition among its customer base and provided free DW watches to a small number of influencers who could show the watch however they liked, use the hashtag #danielwellington, and offer a discount to their followers. This helped the start up to increase its visibility. Second, DW started offering free promotions, including its pick of the day where people could share online their favourite pictures of their DW watches using the hashtag, with some rules for the contest to ensure DW did not lose control of its brand. The best picture of the day won a new watch, and their picture was shared on DW's official Instagram account. While customers received the opportunity for some fame and a free watch, the quid pro quo for DW was thousands of pictures of their watches being posted and shared online. By 2019, DW had 4.9 million followers on Instagram and $173 million in revenue, highlighting the benefits that can accrue from social media influencers.

Equally, social media influencers can also hinder the aspirations of organizations. Naomi Campbell, the famous supermodel, actress, and businesswoman, was approached by Adidas as an influencer to showcase the release of its 350 SPZL kicks. However, this backfired when in 2016 she accidentally shared the promotional instructions that Adidas provided her with. This meant that Adidas lost credibility because audiences did not respond well to their perception of the artificial choreography behind this promotion. It also compromises trust, as audiences questioned whether Campbell really believed in the product or was only promoting the product because she was being paid. The contrast between Adidas prescribing how the influencer should promote the product versus DW empowering influencers to decide themselves is palpable. Given that both businesses operate in many countries and social media messaging via influencers can rapidly spread internationally, this highlights the importance of organizations partnering with influencers authentically to ensure positive rather than negative reputational outcomes.

Cross-border Crises

Organizations can find themselves facing reputation challenges across borders. In 2015, Volkswagen (VW) became embroiled in a scandal that was dubbed 'Dieselgate'. The United States Environment Protection Agency (EPA) issued a notice of violation under the Clean Air Act, having found that many VW cars being sold in America had software installed known as a 'defeat device' that could detect when they were being tested for emissions and change their performance to improve their results. VW ultimately admitted that 11 million cars worldwide were fitted with the defeat device. The seriousness of this crisis was inflamed because of the contrast between VW's noisy marketing campaign that trumpeted the low emissions of its diesel cars and the deceptive and wide-reaching nature of the whole Dieselgate affair. Numerous negative reputational outcomes transpired for VW, which included but were not limited to: a 20% fall in share price on the Frankfurt Stock Exchange following the EPA's announcement; a major decline in car sales compared to the previous year; nearly $5 billion in environmental mitigation and clean-emissions infrastructure costs; the resignation and subsequent indictment of the CEO, Martin Winterkorn, as well as countless vehicle recalls, fines, and legal proceedings in multiple countries.

It is well known that prominent leaders can accrue great rewards for the organizations they serve, but also, at times, unwanted media attention, as the examples of Tony Hayward (of BP), Steve Easterbrook (of McDonald's), and Sir Martin Sorrell (of WPP) illustrate. As well as leaders, employees can also seriously compromise the reputation of organizations. In April 2009, five videos went viral on YouTube that showed a male employee of Domino's Pizza putting cheese up his nose and nasal mucus on sandwiches, while a female employee recorded the prank. Even though this was relatively early days for social media, in the words of Stephanie Clifford in *The New York Times*:

> In a few days, thanks to the power of social media, they ended up with felony charges, more than a million disgusted viewers, and a major company facing a public relations crisis.

This became a reputational crisis for Domino's Pizza because a search on Google and Twitter for Dominos was dominated by the scandal, and the company was forced to issue an apology both on its website and in a YouTube video from the CEO, Patrick Doyle. As I discussed in the first chapter, reputation is about perceptions and Domino's suffered from the actions of its employees, which—given the graphic nature of the video—consequently resulted in customers questioning the quality of its food.

The blurring of boundaries between employee behaviour inside and outside of the workplace, and the potential impact on an organization's reputation is self-evident in the case of a 24-year-old estate agent, Lewis Hughes. In June of 2021, Hughes humiliated Chris Whitty, England's Chief Medical Officer, in '10 seconds of madness' when he asked for a photograph with Whitty; Whitty declined, leading to some antisocial behaviour from Hughes (placing Whitty in a loose headlock), which was filmed. Following footage of the incident being shared on social media, Hughes was swiftly sacked by his employer to avoid any association with Hughes' behaviour and perceptions of the culture of the firm. There are lessons here for all of us about the potential consequences of our conduct outside of the workplace, and lessons for organizations on how the behaviour of their employees outside of work can swiftly impact their reputations.

It is noticeable when employees do compromise the organization's reputation how quickly organizations publicly sever ties and fire their employees, publicly renouncing their behaviour, explaining how it does not reflect the values and culture of their organization. Such announce-ments can become high profile. Or what Enrich and Abrahams (2020) describe in *The New York Times* as the 'disclose-it-and-move-on deco-rum that American corporations have often embraced when confronted with allegations of wrongdoing by senior executives'. Steve Easterbrook, who served as CEO of McDonald's from 2015 to 2019, was dismissed by the Board because of a relationship he had with a staff member, which was in violation of the company's policy. Later in 2020, McDonald's filed a lawsuit against Easterbrook, accusing him of lying, concealing evidence, and fraud, and were seeking to recover his severance pack-age of more than $40 million. This string of events received significant mass media and social media attention. As legal proceedings stretched over several years, greater reputation damage was caused by the under-mining of one of McDonald's key values—integrity—which eroded both McDonald's and Easterbrook's reputations. In December 2021, Easter-brook returned $105 million in cash and stock, which was one of the largest claw-backs in the history of corporate America, and said: 'I apol-ogize to my former co-workers, the board and the company's franchisees and suppliers.'

Reputation damage can also cut across political and business lines. The 1Malaysia Development Berhad (1MDB) scandal in 2016 is con-sidered one of the world's largest financial scandals and was described by officials from the United States Department of Justice as the 'largest single action ever brought under the Kleptocracy Asset Recovery Fund' (Federal Bureau of Investigation 2016). In 2015, the Prime Minister at the time, Najib Razak, was accused of channelling around $700 mil-lion from 1MDB, which is a Malaysian strategic development company wholly owned by the Minister of Finance (Incorporated). After the 2018 general election in which Mahathir Mohamad defeated Najib, he reopened investigations into the 1MDB scandal. Hundreds of handbags and thousands of items of jewellery estimated to be worth $270 million were seized from property linked to Najib. Low Taek Jho, the busi-nessman allegedly behind the 1MBD scandal, was charged with money laundering, although at the time of writing was in exile, and Najib was charged and in 2020 sentenced to twelve years in prison. The reputation fallout of this scandal has been global, with the Malaysian government working with many countries to recover $4.5 billion of 1MDB assets. It has also involved several high-profile political firings, questions over the auditing process, and Goldman Sachs being charged and agreeing to pay $2.9 billion in a settlement with the United States Department of Justice for violating the Foreign Corrupt Practices Act (United States Department of Justice, 2020). This shows the global nature of the scandal and how it cut across multiple political and business lines, with varying levels of reputation ramifications.

Finally, there are not only the risks of reputation damaging events becoming global, but also the risks of organizations being caught in the crossfire with global geopolitical clashes. Geopolitical clashes between the United States and China range from security in the South China Sea, cyber-attacks, the US-Australia-UK submarine deal, climate change, and the alleged treatment of the Uyghur population. Of course, these are just a few examples of how such tensions can add to the complexity of US businesses operating in China and Chinese businesses operating in the US. In terms of the latter, Meng Wanzhou, Deputy Chair of the Board and Chief Financial Officer of Chinese telecommunications multinational Huawei, was arrested in Canada in 2018 on a United States extradition request for fraud and conspiracy to commit fraud, which was formally announced by the US Department of Justice in 2019. The legal challenges extended into 2021 before her release, and demonstrate the blurring of political and business boundaries as well as legal boundaries between the US and Canada. Another example is the murder of Jamal Khashoggi, a US-based journalist and critic of Saudi Arabia's government in the Saudi consulate in Istanbul. This created major tensions between Saudi Arabia and Turkey as well as many other countries such as the US, Canada, France, and the UK, all of whom levied sanctions in addition to other European countries who cancelled arms contracts with Saudi Arabia.

Although these are extreme examples which have received a lot of coverage in the media, they illustrate the complexities for organizations of operating across borders and highlight the blurring of boundaries between individuals and organizations as well as between politics, business, and law. Since the speed and reach of news is so fast via social media, this intensifies the need for organizations to understand and rapidly adapt to the quickly changing global context. What becomes crucial for organizations is ensuring they are not alienating themselves from the competing needs of different stakeholders to maintain a positive reputation.

6

Maintaining Positive Reputations Amid Corruption and Competing Stakeholders

Back in Chapter 1 we looked at how organizations have a variety of stakeholders who need to be identified and managed. The stakeholder capitalism movement illustrates the importance for organizations to engage with a wider set of stakeholders and a need to move beyond rhetoric (fuzzy statements and claims) to action (demonstrable change in behaviours). In Chapter 2, we saw how governments and organizations can hold multiple and competing reputations. Information created and shared on social media is leading to diverse content (some true, some false) and polarizing impressions among audiences, and this is likely to continue. How we navigate managing a variety of stakeholders, with positive actions around polarizing impressions, is explored in this chapter with lessons from a few organizations.

Navigating Corruption and the Needs of Competing Stakeholders: Lessons from Econet in Zimbabwe and Alacrity in India

Resisting corruption means what is right triumphs over powerful people and organizations: it means not giving in when temptation calls and often it means sacrifice. Unfortunately, corruption is a very real part of our modern world, particularly in the industries where politics and money are at play. By way of just one example, in May 2022 the commodity trading and mining company Glencore faced fines of up to $1.5 billion following investigations in the US, UK, and Brazil for bribery and

Reputations at Stake. William S. Harvey, Oxford University Press. © William S. Harvey (2023).
DOI: 10.1093/oso/9780192886521.003.0006

corruption activity to gain preferential access to oil in Cameroon, Equatorial Guinea, Ivory Coast, Nigeria, and South Sudan (Dempsey et al., 2022).

Rama Velamuri, Sankaran Venkataraman, and I researched two firms in India and Zimbabwe who have resisted corruption and built ethical reputations over extended time periods (Velamuri et al., 2017a, 2017b). The first firm, Econet, was founded by Strive Masiyiwa, who approached the Post and Telecommunications Corporation (PTC) of Zimbabwe for a mobile license in 1993. His request was rejected and led to a five-year legal battle against the PTC and the Zimbabwean government. The license was not issued until 1998—two years after PTC had launched its own mobile service and dominated the corporate market, making Econet's contribution to the market a far less viable venture. During the five-year legal battle, there were many occasions where Strive Masiyiwa could have accepted the bribery requests from a small number of individuals in positions of power, but he resisted.

The second firm, Alacrity, in Chennai, India, began as a consulting firm but moved into the construction industry—an industry well known for high levels of corruption, including government intervention—in 1981. Alacrity built an ethical reputation in the construction industry. For twenty years, construction companies had to deal with multiple government departments for each project, including for registration of documents, building regulations, building permits, water and sewerage connections, electricity connection, and oversight of land and construction pricing for tax purposes. There were several instances where Alacrity founder Amol Karnad and the management team refused to bribe public officials because they believed they could thrive without engaging in corrupt practices (Gopinath, 2019). One example cited in *The Economic Times* (1992) noted that the firm refused to pay a bribe to a public official in the state's electricity department, which led to an eight-month delay in completing the project and resulted in Alacrity having to pay customers a penalty of more than $26,000.

What can we learn about navigating competing stakeholders from these two extreme examples in Zimbabwe and India? First, in contexts where there is widespread corruption, both within society and within organizations and teams, there exist disaffected stakeholders who do not map neatly onto traditional stakeholder groups (e.g. investor, employee, regulator, customer, competitor, etc.). In other words, many of these disaffected groups cut across more than one stakeholder category. The fact that these stakeholders have not voiced their dissatisfaction around practices and behaviours does not mean that they will not support organizations who take a lead in committing to ethical values. The opportunity and challenge for organizations is connecting with and understanding what is important for this group of disaffected stakeholders to ensure they mobilize behind their ethical cause.

We find four types of stakeholder responses to ethical behaviour (see Diagram 6.1).

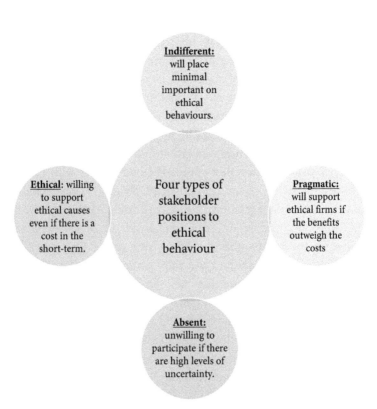

Diagram 6.1 Four Types of Stakeholder Positions to Ethical Behaviour

- First, *indifferent* stakeholders who place minimal emphasis on the ethical behaviours of organizations and are interested only in the outcomes (e.g. return on investment, key performance indicators, and targets), rather than the means through which organizations achieve them, or the wider implications of reaching them for people and society.
- Second, *pragmatic* stakeholders are groups of people who are willing to support ethical organizations so long as the benefit to them is higher than the costs. In other words, they are willing to go so far in supporting ethical causes, but not when they perceive the cost to be too great.
- Third, *absent* stakeholders are not willing to engage in contexts that they consider to be uncertain and therefore are completely disengaged.
- Fourth, *ethical* stakeholders who are committed to supporting ethical organizations even though there may be a cost to them in the short term.

Identifying these categories is important because organizations who are committed to acting ethically in contexts where there is corruption, whether in a country, organization, or team, need to gain the support of pragmatic, absent, and ethical stakeholders to support their cause. Stakeholder groups are not homogeneous in terms of sharing the same values as organizations just because, for example, they are investors, customers, or employees.

Being an ethical organization involves focusing on becoming an ideal organization. The success of organizations, including their reputations, is just as tied up with how ethical they are as how profitable they are.

The first lesson for other organizations is to connect with the pragmatic, absent, and ethical stakeholders and leverage their strong tie and weak tie networks (Granovetter, 1973) to widen the awareness and appeal of an organization's causes. How can organizations frame their ethical commitments, connect with larger groups, and positively impact their reputation? We found that Econet did this through framing its ethical values on the basis of its deep commitment to Christian values. Alacrity, on the other hand, struggled to do this in the same way and resolved to advertise itself in major national newspapers; this came across as self-serving impression management (Velamuri et al., 2017a) and might be described by Rhee and Kim (2012) as a 'superficial response' to managing reputation. The second lesson is to leverage mass media and social media to strengthen the ethical message being conveyed to wider audiences. Reputation claims are considered as more credible when they are made by third parties (Dawkins, 2004), or legitimized in tangible ways that are considered credible (Harvey et al., 2017a). However, it is worth reflecting on which audiences consume what kind of media, because there are variations between different kinds of media (e.g. radio, television, newspapers, social media platforms) as well as within specific media (e.g. TikTok compared to YouTube or CNN compared to the BBC). The strategy organizations take will impact on the kinds of stakeholders they engage with. As Roulet (2020) has illustrated, sometimes by engaging with one stakeholder group, this means alienating yourself from another.

Navigating the Needs of Competing Stakeholders: Lessons from Rio Tinto in Madagascar

Another case study where we can learn about how to manage competing stakeholder demands is from Rio Tinto's operations in Madagascar. This global mining giant was operating in a very poor yet biodiversity-rich country—an operation which could have had catastrophic implications for both the organization's reputation and the landscape on which it carried out its mining. Rowena Olegario, Milena Mueller Santo, and I wanted to know exactly how it navigated the complexities of managing its reputation.

In the mid-1980s, QIT Madagascar Minerals (QMM), a subsidiary of the Rio Tinto Mining group, discovered mineral sand deposits near Fort Dauphin on the south-eastern coast of Madagascar. While sand mining is relatively straightforward, this was one of the most complex projects that Rio Tinto had faced in terms of managing its reputation, given that Madagascar is considered one of the world's twenty-five biodiversity hotspots, with a collection of rich species not found anywhere else in the world. The structure of QMM was also complex, with 80% being owned by Rio Tinto and 20% being owned by the national government of Madagascar. While no local dwelling was located on the mining sites, there were local villages adjacent to the sites and the people relied heavily on the forest and wetlands for their everyday survival needs, from wood for building and cooking, to fruit, game, and medicinal plants. By the mid-1990s, global non-government organizations (NGOs) started to mobilize their objections from the potential extinction of lemur species to the environmental impact in relation to biodiversity depletion and climate change.

In response to the major potential reputation risks, QMM created a full-time environmental and conservation team in Madagascar, led by Manon Vincelette, a foreign engineer who previously worked for Conservation International. QMM sent staff to learn from other complex sites, including Richards Bay in South Africa, and conducted the first Social and Environmental Impact Assessment (SEIA) of its kind in Africa between 1998 and 2001. An independent council was set up as part of the consultation process, which allowed resident objections to lead to the movement of the proposed site and a diversion of a major road away from the town of Fort Dauphin. An independent advisory committee was also set up, which included several major NGOs and biodiversity experts. QMM started partnering with key organizations such as the US Agency for International Development and Key Gardens to develop forest conservation, nurseries, reforestation, and social programmes.

In 2002, a Project Environmental Management Plan (PEMP) was developed for the Mandena site near Fort Dauphin. This outlined QMM's commitment to ecological restoration and reforestation of mined areas and the establishment of a conservation area of littoral forests and wetlands. Almost two decades after starting their exploration, Rio Tinto approved the mining project, with construction starting in 2006 and operations commencing in 2009. QMM's environmental team were charged with achieving a net positive impact on the region's biodiversity.

This was also a major infrastructure project that involved the building of a new port that can handle vessels of up to 60,000 tonnes, new roads, a water treatment plant to enable safe drinking water, and power generation for the mine and residents of Fort Dauphin.

Not surprisingly, there were many stakeholder tensions that emerged. First, inflation following the start of construction. Second, very high expectations around jobs following the mine's construction. Third, inequality between those who were employed by QMM and those who were not. Fourth, resettlement of local people and disputes around the fair cost of recompensing them. QMM sought to proactively engage with two sets of stakeholders: local groups such as the chief of the region, the mayor, and the local people, and global stakeholders such as international NGOs and mass media.

Notwithstanding criticism around the biodiversity initiatives and the engagement with different stakeholders, given the complexities and multiple reputations at stake it would fair to say that QMM has managed its reputations reasonably well over an extended time frame. What are the lessons for other organizations navigating competing stakeholders? First, gaining sufficient expertise in-house can help to bridge the expectation divide between organizations and their stakeholders. Second, understanding what the needs of different stakeholders are and empowering them through independent processes to identify solutions. Third, learning lessons from organizations facing similar challenges in other contexts and not assuming that what has worked for them can succeed for you. Finally, recognizing that while there are risks for both parties of partnering, this can promote learning and help to overcome complex challenges.

Navigating the Needs of Competing Stakeholders: Lessons from Libraries Unlimited

A third example draws on my experience as the Chair of the Board of Libraries Unlimited, which is a UK company limited by guarantee with charitable status seeking to take a new approach to public library services. Serving 750,000 residents, between 2020 and 2021 it had fifty-four libraries (see Diagram 6.2), one mobile library, 80,800 active users, 495,711 books borrowed, 271,196 eBook downloads, 162,135 audiobook

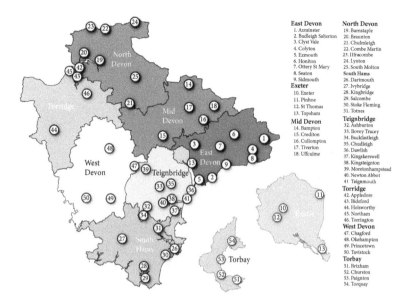

East Devon	North Devon
1. Axminster	19. Barnstaple
2. Budleigh Salterton	20. Braunton
3. Clyst Vale	21. Chulmleigh
4. Colyton	22. Combe Martin
5. Exmouth	23. Ilfracombe
6. Honiton	24. Lynton
7. Ottery St Mary	25. South Molton
8. Seaton	**South Hams**
9. Sidmouth	26. Dartmouth
Exeter	27. Ivybridge
10. Exeter	28. Kingsbridge
11. Pinhoe	29. Salcombe
12. St Thomas	30. Stoke Fleming
13. Topsham	31. Totnes
Mid Devon	**Teignbridge**
14. Bampton	32. Ashburton
15. Crediton	33. Bovey Tracey
16. Cullompton	34. Buckfastleigh
17. Tiverton	35. Chudleigh
18. Uffculme	36. Dawlish
	37. Kingskerswell
	38. Kingsteignton
	39. Moretonhampstead
	40. Newton Abbot
	41. Teignmouth
	Torridge
	42. Appledore
	43. Bideford
	44. Holsworthy
	45. Northam
	46. Torrington
	West Devon
	47. Chagford
	48. Okehampton
	49. Princetown
	50. Tavistock
	Torbay
	51. Brixham
	52. Churston
	53. Paignton
	54. Torquay

Diagram 6.2 Location of Fifty-four Libraries of Libraries Unlimited
Map contains OS data © Crown copyright and database rights 2021

downloads, and 171,346 digital magazine downloads. In 2016, Libraries Unlimited transitioned from being formally part of local government to an independent staff and community owned charity. This has meant that it now has a unique set of stakeholders with whom it engages (see Diagram 6.3).

One of the challenges Libraries Unlimited had been navigating was balancing economic and social value (Hawkings et al., 2019). This is challenging in a context of transition from a library service situated within local government to a company limited by guarantee with charitable status because the operations, reporting, and priorities shift. For example, being independently audited, filing annual accounts with Companies House, and submitting an annual return to the Charity Commission has increased the emphasis on our financial responsibilities alongside our obligations to provide social value to our customers. Social value includes fulfilling the mission to improve and transform people's lives and make a positive difference to the communities it serves in six ways (see Table 6.1).

Diagram 6.3 Libraries Unlimited Stakeholders

One of the challenges of the changing balance of economic and social value is that it can disrupt stakeholder engagement. For example, librarians generally do not have commercial training and so being asked to operate within a commercial context can be an affront to their training, experience, and professional identity. At the same time, the Board and Senior Management Team needed a shift in how libraries operated: events that run at a loss or additional services that do not sufficiently generate revenue at scale could adversely affect the bottom line and viability of the organization. Then of course there are the expectations of commissioners and funders who expect the delivery of a particular quality of library service as well as 750,000 local residents who are eligible to use the service free of charge. They, of course, will have views about what

Table 6.1 Libraries Unlimited Mission and Six Core Purposes

Mission: Improve and transform people's lives and make a positive difference to the communities we serve

Purpose 1: Promoting and encouraging a love of reading

Purpose 2: Promoting free access to information to help people in their everyday lives

Purpose 3: Inspiring people of all ages to learn, imagine, create, succeed, and realize their potential

Purpose 4: Offering a welcoming space to meet, socialize, learn, read, and enjoy new experiences

Purpose 5: Guiding and supporting people to explore and connect to the wider world

Purpose 6: Supporting the health and wellbeing of individuals and communities

---

services they should be entitled to access for free (e.g. books, magazines, ebooks, audiobooks, computers with internet, a business and intellectual property centre), and those for which they would need to pay (e.g. room hire, late return fees, events, and additional services). A further complexity is that some libraries have their own Friends Groups, which in some cases are separate charities representing the interests of a particular library. Inevitably, these Friends Groups have their own sets of priorities focused on a library which may vary in their alignment with the strategy of Libraries Unlimited. These examples illustrate how the expectations of stakeholders can vary and how the role of a board and an executive team is to understand these varying expectations and to formulate a strategy accordingly. This becomes particularly significant in a rapidly changing context.

Strategies are great in theory, but they seldom go according to plan. As fellow Board member Morgen Witzel and I have described, the process of formulating a strategy can create friction, particularly if the wider context is experiencing stress. However, in the context of the COVID-19 pandemic stakeholder friction can also generate positive outcomes (Harvey and Witzel, 2020). In early 2020, as Chair of the Board I started the process of revising our strategy, given that we had recently appointed a new Chief Executive and several new Board members and were now

Table 6.2 Terminology when Formulating a Strategy at Libraries Unlimited

Mission	What business the organization is in (and what it isn't) both now and projecting into the future
Purpose	Inspiring staff to do great work and expressing the organization's impact on the lives of others that it serves
Goals	The ongoing aspirations of the organization
Values	The desired behaviours of staff within the organization
Strategy	Doing something new, building on what is already being done, and/or reacting to emerging opportunities
Measures	Assurance that what the Board hears and observes aligns with the organization's purpose, aspirations, and values

established as an organization outside of local government. One of the starting points of this process was clarifying terminology, as in my experience in business using terms such as mission, purpose, goals, values, strategy, and measures can mean very different things to different people, which can create confusion and potentially conflict. Table 6.2 summarizes the agreed terminology.

At the Board meeting in April 2020, the Board agreed on the terminology and was in the process of formulating a strategy. In particular, the senior management team was tasked with the creation of a strategy given their knowledge of the operational detail on which the Board should feed back and challenge where appropriate due to their more distant perspective on the organization. My view as Chair was that the Board should not approve the strategy unless it was willing to own and support it. In the words of John Sutherland (2020), the executive generally have more time, knowledge, and experience to create the strategy, but the Board should take the responsibility to understand, test, and endorse the strategy.

Around the time of this Board strategy process, the COVID-19 pandemic forced Libraries Unlimited to close its buildings and reduce its services. It soon became apparent that while some libraries might reopen in the Summer of 2020, there was not going to be a swift reopening. It was clear that the pandemic was already having a powerful social impact on our communities including rising unemployment, growing gaps in education attainment, poorer families being hardest hit, and a steep rise in physical and mental health issues. These are all issues that directly relate to our six core purposes (see Table 6.1) and do not neatly map onto one or a small number of stakeholder groups. The timing and process of library closure and reopening inevitably created stakeholder conflict. For example, as a Board we were torn between our statutory obligations to our commissioners and funders around providing a vital educational, social, and health service to our communities and customers. At the same time, providing such comprehensive service created risk and pressure on our outstanding staff and volunteers, without whom there would be no service.

The combination of pushback on our strategy and a global pandemic catalysed the task and finish group to swiftly change course and pace (Harvey and Witzel, 2020). Within four weeks, Witzel had held personal conversations with the Chief Executive, different Board members, and various operational managers, followed by a task and finish group discussion to summarize and approve the next steps. What culminated was a set of five core objectives (see Diagram 6.4) that was approved by the task and finish group, brought to the Board, and unanimously signed off. This enabled the executive team to work immediately on their operational plans to deliver on these objectives, which the Board could subsequently measure. Notwithstanding the different stakeholder challenges that Libraires Unlimited have faced, these objectives have

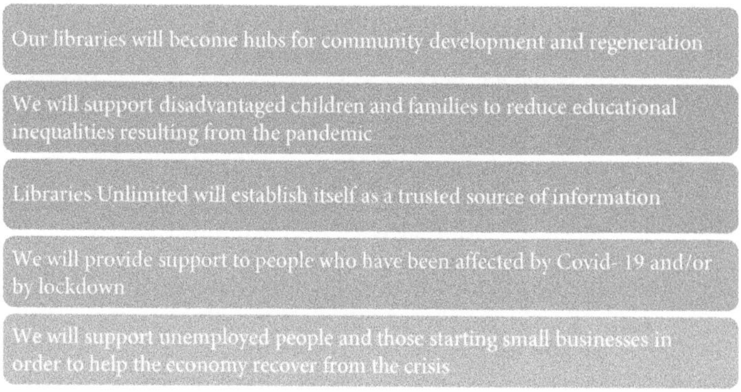

Our libraries will become hubs for community development and regeneration

We will support disadvantaged children and families to reduce educational inequalities resulting from the pandemic

Libraries Unlimited will establish itself as a trusted source of information

We will provide support to people who have been affected by Covid-19 and/or by lockdown

We will support unemployed people and those starting small businesses in order to help the economy recover from the crisis

Diagram 6.4 Five Core Objectives

Table 6.3 Stakeholder Quotations

Stakeholder	Quotation
Customers	'Thank you for your help to get online. This library has been a life saver.'
	'The service is a lifeline.'
	'I can't thank you enough for your kindness over the last year; it has made lockdown so much more bearable than it would have been.'
	'My daughter was feeling quite isolated and low during the lockdown in March to June 2020. As a new mum, she was missing community connection and baby groups, which she had hoped to belong to with her first baby. I suggested when the library reopened that she joined. Her experience was so positive, she was amazed it was a free service and was blown over by the care the staff gave her. A big thank you to all staff for not just offering a book service but such a positive experience.'
Volunteers	'I have made new friends and it makes me feel that I am contributing towards my community in some small way.'
	'It helped me to meet and make friends after I moved here in 2016 not knowing anyone.'
	'I love the interaction with members of staff and the locals and look forward to my time with them. I enjoy helping people which gives me satisfaction to see them leave smiling and with a question resolved.'
	'I have gained confidence, feel useful and appreciated, made new friends and enjoy being part of a team.'
	'I like feeling useful and being part of a group of people with common interests. Being part of the local community, having my knowledge valued. I'm learning new things all the time.'
Staff	'The investment by The British Library in Libraries Unlimited in September 2020 has allowed the recruitment of 3 full time individuals to the BIPC and the new team has moved at an incredible pace to build an amazing programme that continues to grow week on week, providing much needed business support to our local communities.'
	'We have a man who lives in a camper van locally and therefore doesn't have any WiFi. He is in regularly when we are open doing his paperwork for his business and announced to us that he had sent his first invoice in the summer using the library WiFi. He is so pleased with the service that he regularly leaves a donation.'

Source: Libraries Unlimited (2021)

enabled the organization to deliver an excellent service to multiple stakeholders within a highly challenging context, as a few examples from different stakeholders show (see Table 6.3).

A Summary of Navigating Competing Stakeholders

Building on the three different examples above, what are the lessons for how to navigate the needs of different stakeholders?

- Invest in gaining sufficient expertise in-house to bridge the expectation divide between organizations and their stakeholders.
- Develop an understanding of what the needs of different stakeholders are and empower them through independent processes to identify solutions.
- Learn from organizations facing similar challenges in other contexts and don't assume what has worked for them will work for you.
- Recognize that while there are risks for both parties of partnering, this can promote learning and help to overcome complex challenges.
- Connect with the pragmatic, absent, and ethical stakeholders and leverage networks to widen the awareness and appeal of an organization's causes.
- Leverage mass and social media to strengthen the ethical message to wider audiences.
- Clarify and communicate with stakeholders around terminology to ensure consistent understanding.

The three sets of examples (Econet in Zimbabwe and Alacrity in India; Rio Tinto in Madagascar; Libraries Unlimited in the UK) demonstrate very different economic sectors (telecommunications, housing, mining, and libraries) and geographic contexts (Zimbabwe, India, Madagascar, and the UK). However, all these organizations faced difficult and ongoing challenges in relation to managing the perceptions and expectations of their stakeholders. Often the different expectations of their stakeholders were not aligned, which adds to the complexity of not only being aware of the perceptions of stakeholders, but responding to their needs in a considered manner.

This is timely given the momentum towards stakeholder capitalism where organizations of different structures (and not just corporations) need to substantively engage in their wider responsibilities, for example in relation to climate change, biodiversity depletion, social inequality, community disconnection, and other challenges that relate to people and the planet. For organizations to do this in a meaningful way, there needs to be a shift from rhetoric to reality. We have seen a lot of organizations make warm statements about their environmental and social commitments and read lots of glossy publications about what they are doing, but often there has been relatively little evidence of substantive action. This requires organizations to reflect and reconsider their purpose, which lies at the heart of the stakeholder capital movement. Purpose is the life blood of an organization and aligning it with values and society is a tricky business which we will explore in the next chapter.

7

Aligning Purpose and Values

In the opening chapter, I referenced how stakeholder capitalism is starting to gain traction in the business community, with prominent, influential organizations and outlets (such as the Business Roundtable, the British Academy, the World Economic Forum, Harvard Business Review, and the Ellen MacArthur Foundation) encouraging a rethinking of purpose. In the second chapter, I noted that pressure is mounting on governments from the UN's annual Conference of the Parties (COP) and from grassroot organizations such as the Extinction Rebellion and Insulate Britain (who are using civil resistance tactics) to increase ambition and catalyse change. These movements are not just environmental but social and economic too, with other examples including Black Lives Matter, Occupy Wall Street, #MeToo, and the *gilets jaunes* movements. Hence, these wider events speak to broader societal sentiments and movements that relate to environmental, social, and economic issues.

In the previous chapter, I described *purpose* as 'inspiring staff to do great work and expressing the organization's impact on the lives of others that it serves' and *values* as 'the desired behaviours of staff within the organization' (see Table 6.2). A reputational risk for organizations is when their purpose becomes disconnected from wider societal trends. In other words, there is a societal-purpose gap that can lead to external criticism.

Sometimes an organization's mission statement can act as a bridge between societal trends and the organization's activities. However, Facebook's (2021) mission to 'Give people the power to build community and bring the world closer together' did not stop it from facing what *The Economist* (2021a) described as 'nearing a reputational point of no return', particularly in relation to ongoing criticism around the negative impact the social media platform is having on the mental health of many of its users. This presumably accelerated an announcement by the

Reputations at Stake. William S. Harvey, Oxford University Press. © William S. Harvey (2023).
DOI: 10.1093/oso/9780192886521.003.0007

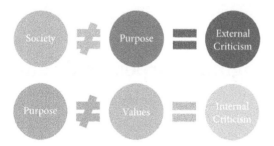

Diagram 7.1 Misalignment of Society, Purpose, and Values

CEO, Mark Zuckerberg, to change the name of its holding company from Facebook to Meta. While this was couched as a reflection of the firm's strategic ambitions to build the 'metaverse'—a digital world over the existing world through virtual and augmented reality—the timing of the announcement revealed a desire to protect reputation in the face of mounting regulatory and PR challenges (Paul, 2021).

Another reputational risk for organizations is when their purpose does not align with their values; if the words and statements the Board and Executive support do not connect with employees, this can lead to internal criticism. Hence, to avoid external and internal criticism, organizations need to have alignment between society, purpose, and values (see Diagram 7.1).

Given that I have discussed societal trends in Chapters 1 to 4, let us now focus on purpose and values and their alignment in this chapter.

Purpose

In the last few decades there have been many examples of privileging the corporate shareholder. However, this model is starting to be challenged. In 2019, the Business Roundtable, a powerful group that represents the largest companies in the United States, released a revised statement on the purpose of a corporation (see Diagram 7.2).

What is noticeable in the statement is the two references to the importance of stakeholders: 'we share a fundamental commitment to all of our stakeholders' and 'Each of our stakeholders is essential'. A year

While each of our individual companies serves its own corporate purpose, we share a fundamental commitment to all of our stakeholders. We commit to:

- *Delivering value to our customers. We will further the tradition of American companies leading the way in meeting or exceeding customer expectations.*

- *Investing in our employees. This starts with compensating them fairly and providing important benefits. It also includes supporting them through training and education that help develop new skills for a rapidly changing world. We foster diversity and inclusion, dignity and respect.*

- *Dealing fairly and ethically with our suppliers. We are dedicated to serving as good partners to the other companies, large and small, that help us meet our missions.*

- *Supporting the communities in which we work. We respect the people in our communities and protect the environment by embracing sustainable practices across our businesses.*

- *Generating long-term value for shareholders, who provide the capital that allows companies to invest, grow and innovate. We are committed to transparency and effective engagement with shareholders.*

Each of our stakeholders is essential. We commit to deliver value to all of them, for the future success of our companies, our communities and our country.

Diagram 7.2 Excerpt From the Business Roundtable's (2019) Statement on the Purpose of a Corporation earlier, the British Academy (2018), the UK's national academy for the humanities and social sciences, published a report on 'Reforming Business for the 21st Century', which called for a reconceptualization of the corporation around purpose. The report is clear that corporate purpose should further the interests of multiple groups:

> Corporate purposes are the reasons a corporation is created and exists, what it seeks to do and what it aspires to become. They reflect the contribution it wishes to make in furthering the interests of its customers, communities and societies and they are the basis on which relations of trust are created in business. They are distinct from the consequential implications for the corporation's profitability and shareholder returns.
>
> (British Academy, 2018: 10–11)

As the British Academy argues, the corporate purpose should lie at the centre of why a corporation exists, whereas profit is one of many outcomes of corporate purpose.

Corporate purpose has gained wider media traction and is the topic of many recent high-profile articles including a company's core reason for being (Gast et al., 2020), businesses placing purpose at the centre of their strategies (Malnight et al., 2019), what companies are for (*The Economist*, 2019), and a manifesto on corporate governance to enable directors to lead sustainable purposeful businesses (IoD, 2019). Many other organizations have been publicly discussing purpose, including Accenture, Ernst and Young, the World Economic Forum, and Forbes. While there has been a lot of noise about purpose, as I explore elsewhere (Harvey, 2021b) it is worth understanding what businesses are doing (rather than claiming) in relation to addressing purpose.

Business Action on Purpose

There has been growing cross-sector initiative from businesses around the issue of purpose. The Enacting Purpose Initiative, which is a multi-institution partnership between the University of Oxford, the University of California at Berkeley, BCG BrightHouse, EOS at Federated

Hermes, and the British Academy, has written two reports on the purpose of the corporation. The first report provides a framework for Directors on how to enact purpose (Enacting Purpose Initiative, 2020). The second report targets Directors and Investors around how to build common ground for advancing sustainable capitalism (Enacting Purpose Initiative, 2021).

One indicator of positive initiatives by organizations is to look at rankings where employees nominate their organization. As with all rankings, there are limitations with the methodologies of how organizations are judged, and opportunities for organizations and their members to game them. Nevertheless, they do give an indicator of some good practices.

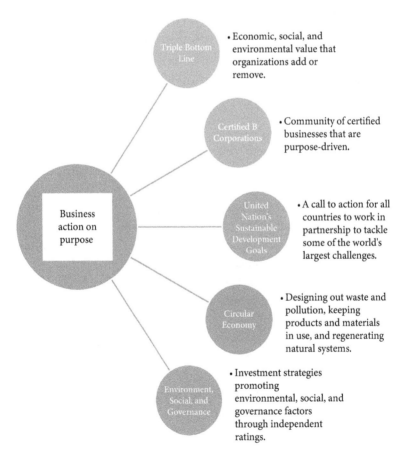

Diagram 7.3 Five Examples of Business Action on Purpose

Glassdoor, for example, has an annual ranking focused on mission, culture, people, and transparency. In 2022, Nvidia came top in the US, ServiceNow in the UK, bioMérieux in France, and Salesforce in Germany (Glassdoor, 2022).

There are at least five interrelated examples of what businesses are doing in relation to purpose: they can engage with the triple bottom line (TBL), Certified B Corporations (B Corps), the UN's sustainable development goals (SDGs), the circular economy (CE), and investment in environmental, social, and corporate governance (ESG) (see Diagram 7.3). This is not an exhaustive list, but it highlights some of the different and overlapping ways that businesses are demonstrating action on purpose—by adhering to a certain set of standards.

1. The first example is the triple bottom line (TBL), which is a term allegedly introduced by John Elkington. He argued that the TBL is about the economic, environmental, and social values that organizations can add or remove, which has some similarities with stakeholder theory (Freeman et al., 2010). There are also parallels with corporate social responsibility given the emphasis on taking environmental, social, and financial issues seriously. Despite some criticism, the inclusion of accountancy language has been important for gaining buy-in within business circles (Norman and MacDonald, 2004) because it enables businesses to formally account for its activity and performance around economic, social, and environmental issues. It is also likely to gain traction given the range of economic, health, environmental, and social challenges such as global financial crises, pandemics, climate change, and social movements such as #MeToo and Black Lives Matter.

2. Another example is Certified B Corporations (B Corps). Businesses can become part of a community of certified businesses that are purpose-driven through the collective expectation to meet the 'highest standards of verified social and environmental performance, public transparency, and legal accountability to balance profit and purpose' (B Corporation, 2021: np). B Corps consider the value of a wider set of stakeholders, including employees and

community members. A classic example is the outdoors company, Patagonia, who introduced a 1% earth tax on itself in the 1980s to support grassroots environmental organizations. 70% of its products are made from recycled materials with the goal to be using 100% renewable or recycled materials by 2025.

3. An organization can also subscribe to the United Nation's (UN) sustainable development goals (SDGs). These SDGs are a call to action for all governments around the world to work in partnership with organizations and other countries to address some of the world's largest challenges (United Nations, 2021). The SDGs can help organizations to participate in focused activity. The Canadian national telecommunications company Telus, for example, created a network of outreach clinics and affordable internet and mobile phone plans for vulnerable and marginalized Canadian communities (Klar, 2019). Cynics of these kinds of initiatives suggest that this is just an example of corporate greenwashing, which is the rhetoric of diverting sustainability claims to cover up a questionable environmental record. Research of 700 global companies by PwC (2018: 3) suggests that some of the rhetoric is beginning to translate to action. For example, from the survey 72% mentioned SDGs, 27% included them in their business strategy, and 19% were mentioned in the CEO or Chair report in relation to the business strategy, performance, or outlook. There is some substance behind this claim. For example, the day before the UN's 26th Conference of the Parties (COP26) opened in Glasgow on 31 October 2021, the edition of *The Economist* pictured three emperor penguins standing on an ice floe with the caption 'COP-Out'. Not surprisingly, there was a lot of focus on climate change around that time. What was noticeable, however, was out of the 100-page publication (including front and back covers,) thirty-seven pages included climate-related adverts and advocacy from a plethora of organizations, covering energy, technology, asset management, investment banking, insurance, and accountancy—clearly an indication of how businesses are striving to support the UN's SDGs, but also a warning of heightened greenwashing activity.

4. The circular economy (CE), another example of how businesses engage in purpose, aims to redefine growth, focusing on positive societal benefits, through three core principles:

  (i) Designing out waste and pollution
  (ii) Keeping products and materials in use
  (iii) Regenerating natural systems
  (Ellen MacArthur Foundation, 2021).

Peter Hopkinson and I have argued that the CE movement has gained momentum among businesses in the last decade for four reasons (Hopkinson and Harvey, 2019: 69):

  (a) A powerful vision of the value of transitioning from a linear economy to a circular economy, and the wider benefits that this can bring to nature, the economy, and society.
  (b) A well-known and influential leader in Dame Ellen MacArthur who has gained attention and respect across the business and political spectrum.
  (c) Partnering with prominent organizations from different sectors (e.g. BlackRock, Ikea, and Unilever) and organizations who have influence (e.g. McKinsey & Company and the World Economic Forum).
  (d) Providing a visualization to help others to understand the movement. For example, the Ellen MacArthur Butterfly diagram helps governments and organizations to understand the concept of the circular economy so that they can reflect on how to apply it in their own contexts.

5. The final example of businesses engaging in purpose relates to their investments in environmental, social, and governance (ESG) issues. Environmental could include issues such as energy consumption and waste; social factors could include how businesses engage with their workforce and promote fairness, diversity, and inclusion practices; governance could include factors related to leadership, decision-making, ethics, and compliance. ESG is a broad movement that describes the myriad steps that organizations are taking to evaluate their collective approach to

environmental, social, and governance issues. This movement stems from the UN's emphasis on corporate social responsibility, which gained traction but also a lot of cynicism because while organizations were strong on impression management, they were weak on evidencing. Although there are many examples of measurement and evaluation of ESG, the emphasis today appears to be more on measurement and action than impression management and branding. Having said this, there is evidence that action is still falling short of the rhetoric (Jenkins, 2022).

The above five examples highlight the different and overlapping ways that organizations are engaging with purpose. However, we need to understand how organizational purpose can align with their values and translate into desirable actions and behaviours. This leads us to our discussion about values.

Organizational Values and How They Can Be Internalized Within Organizations

Organizational values describe the characteristics of organizations (Chatman, 1991). These values are important for helping employees to make sense of their workplaces and for guiding their behaviour (Bourne and Jenkins, 2013). They are a central component of organizational culture, which impacts on the performance and reputation of the organization (Barney, 1986). Given the importance of values, how can they be internalized within organizations? Drawing on research with my colleagues Sharina Osman and Marwa Tourky (Harvey et al., 2021c), I share an example of a Malaysian hospital.

Creating Values in HKL

We conducted research in a hospital that was created in the mid-1990s in Malaysia that we refer to as HKL to preserve its anonymity. The founder and CEO of HKL played a central role at the outset in creating the values of the hospital, which aligned with its purpose of delivering a premium healthcare service with a personalized experience for patients. It is worth highlighting that Malaysia scores 100 on power distance, meaning that 'people accept a hierarchical order in which everybody has a place and which needs no further justification' (Hofstede Insights (2021: np). However, employees of the hospital did not accept the values that the CEO and senior leadership team identified. Our interviews found that employees did not recognize how the values that were identified related to them and their work. This was an important inflection point for the leadership team, recognizing that creating organizational values was not a tick box tokenistic exercise that can be imposed from above.

The push back from employees led to a complete rethink of how employees could coproduce the hospital's values through workshops, consultations, and working groups. The goal of this exercise was to ensure there was alignment between the organization's purpose (e.g. the strategy), its values (e.g. the guiding principles for employees), and its identity (e.g. an agreed understanding of 'who we are as an organization' that guides employee behaviours) (see Diagram 7.4). What transpired was a diffusion process that engaged employees at different levels, rather than being entirely top-down from the senior leadership team or a bottom-up approach from employees.

The values that were agreed upon included care and respect, being passionate, accountability, service excellence, anticipation, team spirit, changing and growing, quality and safety, and social responsibility. These values were not just vacuous statements preserved for noticeboards, websites, or meetings, but guiding principles that form the basis of how employees identify with the organization, including a set of corresponding value-based behaviours. It is less important understanding *what* the values are because every organization has its own unique set. What is more important is understanding the process of *how* values are created and embedded as this is likely to determine whether values are for show or for real.

Organizational Purpose	• Strategy
Organizational Values	• Guiding principles
Organizational Identity	• Behaviours

Diagram 7.4 Alignment of Purpose, Values, and Identities

Based on our research within the hospital, we found that for values to be internalized they need to be effectively created, communicated, and enacted. Values which are only created by senior leaders run the risk of disengaging other members of the organization. Values which are effectively created but poorly communicated are likely to be lost among employees. Values which are effectively created and communicated but not enacted through behaviours creates a problem of legitimacy where certain segments of the organization understand the values but are unable or unwilling to enact them. We found that values can be internalized within organizations through a process that we summarize as LIME: Leaders, Internalize, Managers, and Employees (Harvey et al., 2021c) (see Diagram 7.5).

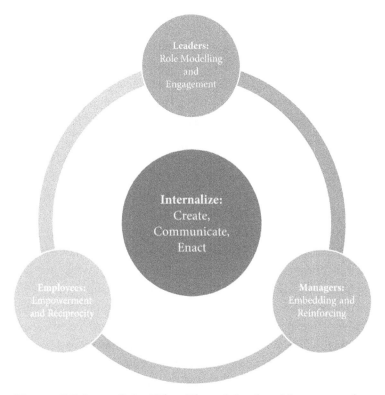

Diagram 7.5 Internalizing Values Through Leaders, Managers, and Employees

The process of internalization requires creating, communicating, and enactment of values. However, for this to be achieved certain behaviours are required from leaders, managers, and employees.

Leaders need to exhibit role model behaviours and engage different members of the organization in adopting and internalizing the values. Managers need to help embed and reinforce the values within their departments and divisions. Employees need to be empowered to enact and reciprocate those values. We found the outcome of the LIME process was three interactive processes:

1. Positive internal beliefs around what the organization considers important.
2. Employee behaviours that align with the organization's values.
3. Positive internal perceptions of the organization.

When we interviewed in-patients and out-patients of the hospital, many examples were shared of how they had personally experienced and benefitted from employee behaviours that aligned to the organization's values. Hence, effectively internalizing values can connect the organization's purpose and identity as well as build its reputation among internal and external stakeholders.

Another example of where these three processes were effectively embedded in an organization was described by Paul Polman, the former CEO of Unilever. In his book he documents a stressful time involving intense pressure to sell when Unilever was faced with the threat of a hostile takeover bid in February 2017 from Kraft Heinz, an organization controlled by Berkshire Hathaway and 3G Capital (*Net Positive*, Polman and Winston, 2021). Polman and Winston argue that one of the reasons the takeover failed was because critics underestimated how different stakeholders, including the leadership team, the board, NGOs, and unions, cared about how Unilever approached business in a responsible and long-term manner, which was in stark contrast to perceptions of the short-term value emphasis of Kraft Heinz. Unilever's proactive management of reputation over time played a valuable role in helping their organization respond to a threat. Aligning purpose and values is the keystone for organizations being resistant to different levels of threat.

This chapter has focused on the importance of aligning purpose and values. The alignment of society and purpose can help to stave off external criticism, while alignment of purpose and values can help to stave off internal criticism. Or, in a more positive framing: alignment of society, purpose, and values can help to guide behaviours as well as build and sustain reputation among internal and external stakeholders. This kind of proactive management of reputation over time is important because at some point all organizations face different kinds of threats, even those who are performing well.

8

Responding to Threats

Whether we like it or not, all of us and every organization faces different gradations of threat to our reputation. This could be a small-scale threat around the competency or legitimacy of a leader, a middle-level threat around the strategy and future trajectory of an organization, or a large-scale threat that questions the culture or future existence of an entire industry. It is overly simplistic to label threats as small, medium, or large, but some examples can serve to illustrate how they can range in scale, but cut across politics, business, and society.

At an individual level, in October 2021 the President of Brazil, Jair Bolsonaro, received damning criticism from senators following his handling of the coronavirus pandemic of 2020–2021. A senate panel backed a 1,300-page report calling for charges against the President, including crimes against humanity, after 600,000 deaths had been reported from the pandemic. Despite the President's response that he was 'guilty of absolutely nothing' and the report being handled by Bolsonaro's appointed chief prosecutor, the accusations of crimes against humanity, incitement to crime, falsification of documents, and violation of social rights have caused significant reputation damage for the President in the build-up to the 2022 general election, which he narrowly lost.

Another individual level example is the Costa Concordia cruise ship disaster of January 2012. There were 4,229 people on board the ship when it struck an underwater rock, capsized, and sank off the Italian island of Giglio in the Mediterranean, tragically killing thirty-two people. It took the captain of the ship one hour and three minutes from the collision to raise the general alarm, despite the fact the chief engineer had informed personnel on the bridge after ten minutes that two of the watertight compartments were flooded, meaning the stability of the ship was compromised. The captain was later sentenced to sixteen years

Reputations at Stake. William S. Harvey, Oxford University Press. © William S. Harvey (2023).
DOI: 10.1093/oso/9780192886521.003.0008

in prison: ten years for manslaughter, five years for causing the ship-wreck, and one year for abandoning his passengers. Had he, as a leader, responded swiftly, disaster—as well as reputation damage—could have been avoided.

At an organizational level, McKinsey & Company has faced several threats to its reputation. First, signing off on its biggest ever contract in Africa at the end of 2015 which *The New York Times* dubbed as 'the biggest mistake in McKinsey's nine-decade history' (Bogdanich and Forsythe, 2018), and which turned out to be illegal. Second, the report that McKinsey & Company had produced a short document revealing the public perception of particular economic policies, including detail-ing three individuals who were driving much of the negative news of Saudi Arabia (Kolhatkar, 2018). After the report was created, one of the individuals (Khalid al-Alkami) was arrested and a brother (Omar Abdulaziz) was imprisoned, once again casting suspicion on McKinsey & Company. Following a barrage of online criticism and a damning report in *The New York Times*, McKinsey & Company made a pub-lic statement denying the accusations. Third, a series of lawsuits from fifty US states regarding the company's advice to Purdue Pharma LP on how to maximize the sales of the addictive painkiller OxyContin, which has contributed to part of the country's opioid epidemic (Condon and Torres, 2021). McKinsey & Company paid more than $600 million in 2021 to resolve claims across the US in relation to its role in the US opi-oid epidemic, but denied any wrongdoing or unlawfulness. Regardless of the truth (remember reputation is perception not fact), these recur-ring prominent stories impact on perceptions of McKinsey & Company and suggest that they are more than isolated examples and may actu-ally reflect something more profound related to culture and leadership within the firm (Edgecliffe-Johnson et al., 2021).

At a sector level, in April 2021 a European Super League plan for twenty clubs to compete in an elite football league was presented. Excite-ment and drama were promised, with some of the clubs interested including Chelsea, Liverpool, Manchester City, Manchester United, Barcelona, Real Madrid, AC Milan, and Juventus. However, within a few days of the story breaking the initiative ended in what was described as a 'spectacular own goal' (*The Economist*, 2021b). While the organizers outlined a financial rationale for investors and owners (particularly the opportunity for greater revenue and a reduction of financial risk through relegation), they had not secured the support of other important stakeholders such as managers, players, fans, broadcasters, journalists, and governments. In the UK, even the Prime Minister weighed in, vowing to do 'everything I can to give this ludicrous plan a straight red'. The loud and outspoken criticism from different groups contributed to the whole initiative collapsing. Football club owners then found themselves having to publicly apologize for not consulting and for being wildly out of touch with the sentiments of many different groups. This is a lesson for organizations in the potential consequences of focusing on only a narrow group of stakeholders and the speed with which threats can occur when they do not understand or engage with the perceptions of different groups.

Having identified that threats can occur at the individual, organizational, and sector level, let us look at what organizations can do to mitigate these threats through two research projects: first, a global management consulting firm that experienced a disconnect between its reputation and identity (Harvey et al., 2017a); second, a meat processing company trying to improve its leadership and culture within a challenging working environment and sector (Harvey et al., 2014).

Reputation and Identity Conflict in Management Consulting

Let us refer to a global management consulting firm as ConsultRep, researched by Tim Morris, Milena Mueller Santos, and me, and whose reputation was of interest to us (Harvey et al., 2017a). ConsultRep has operated for over fifty years, with several thousand employees across more than fifty offices worldwide. When we conducted interviews, focus groups, and observations, and examined secondary sources, we observed a disconnect between the firm's identity claims ('who we think we are and why we are distinctive') and its reputation ('how others perceive our identity claims in relation to our reputation'). To some extent this is not surprising because all organizations will experience a gap between their identity and reputation. However, what is more pressing

Table 8.1 Types of Identity-reputation Gaps and Responses

Extent of identity and reputation gap	Description of context	Organizational action required
Small	Satisfactory: close alignment of perceptions between internal and external stakeholders	Management: ensure ongoing alignment
Medium	Problem: gap in perceptions between internal and external stakeholders	Repair: reduce gap and avoid escalation
Large	Crisis: fundamental disconnection between internal and external perceptions	Recover: reset perceptions to avoid untenable position

is understanding the extent of the gap between their identity and reputation. Table 8.1 illustrates three different levels of identity-reputation gaps (small, medium, and large), with corresponding descriptions (satisfactory, problem, crisis) and action required (management, repair, recover). In the case of ConsultRep, this was a medium level of gap that was neither superficial nor existential, but was a problem for the firm that required repairing to avoid escalation.

At the time of our research, the firm was consistently ranked by external validators as a top ten global management consulting firm and had been approached several times by at least three of the big four accounting firms to merge. Its identity claims focused on being European, entrepreneurial, and offering strategy with pragmatism, whereas its reputation was centred around restructuring and providing pragmatic solutions. Both internal stakeholders (e.g. consultants and senior consultants) and external stakeholders (e.g. clients, non-clients, and competitors) did not believe these identity claims, which created a gap between identity and reputation. Many of the people we spoke to suggested that the claims were meaningless or inconsistent with their own experience. This triggered ConsultRep to respond through three approaches. First, shifting the messaging through individual consultants rather than via corporate branding, which professional service firms tend to struggle to land successfully with clients (Harvey and Mitchell, 2015).

Second, building trust in their claims through evidencing via thought leadership channels (e.g. blogs, tweets, interviews, videos, infographics, etc.). Third, through emphasizing the value that they provide to clients by over-delivering. The first two approaches seemed to be effective over time in buffering the gap between its identity claims and reputation. However, the third approach was not particularly well received by clients because although they appreciated consultants going the extra mile, often this came as across as needy and desperate to please as opposed to signalling their desired identity. Nevertheless, the outcome of the above response was a buffered identity-reputation gap (see Diagram 8.1) and a compromised position around strategic operations, which was a hybrid of ConsultRep's desire to be a major strategy consulting firm and its building on its historical strengths around implementation.

The lesson for other organizations, particularly professional service firms, is to avoid an overly top-down approach when projecting your identity. This needs to be cocreated with employees and with trusted outsiders to ensure they buy in. Although websites, social media, and digital displays can reach large audiences, if the actual work of the consultants is not aligned then the messaging and credibility is lost. However, this can be salvaged if there is clear evidencing of any claims through the work that consultants deliver, through the endorsement of third parties (i.e. clients), and via relevant and high quality thought leadership[1] activity.

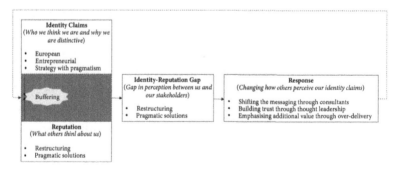

Diagram 8.1 Reducing the Gap Between Identity Claims and Reputation

---

[1] My colleagues and I have defined thought leadership as 'Knowledge from a trusted, eminent and authoritative source that is actionable and provides valuable solutions for stakeholders' (Harvey et al., 2021d: 11).

Leadership and Cultural Change in Meat Processing

A more than thirty-five-years old Australian family-owned fresh food and meal solutions business called Beak and Johnston (B&J) also mitigated threats to their reputation in 2013. Stuart Parry, Paul Vorbach, and I started researching B&J when it was performing well with sales exceeding AUD $300 million, with a stretched target of becoming a billion-dollar company by 2020 (Harvey et al., 2014). We observed two specific threats that B&J faced that are common to many organizations. First, leadership: B&J was founded by David Beak, an Englishman and Oxford graduate who was the fourth generation of his family to work in the meat industry. Having started and grown the business as founder and CEO, he was looking at how to manage his succession. Second, B&J's culture: its sub-optimal communication and accountability of managers was flagged as a threat to the future success of the business. To explore these themes in more depth, we were granted access to interview senior leaders, managers, and employees, and were permitted to observe behaviour at the main Greenacre site and dynamics at senior leadership team meetings and away days.

With the leadership challenge, Beak recognized that his Board had to drag him away from micromanaging the business. Assessment of his leadership style as well as those of the senior management team by the American Management Association DISC Survey™ came back as dominant and overly driven by results, which contributed to 'why we were a dysfunctional team'. This triggered an overhaul in the senior leadership team with subsequent recruitment and selection being driven by a desire to attract and retain leaders with a diverse range of personalities and skillsets. Beak also looked at his own leadership style, reflecting on how he could be 'interfering, visionary, driven, competitive, obsessive, never satisfied, and restless', which led to hiring an executive coach to help him and his senior leadership team to reflect on their long-term development as leaders and as a leadership team. This reflective process revealed leaders that were overly distant from the challenges and realities of the factory floor—something that many organizations suffer from. Beak was inspired by an article in *Harvard Business Review* written by Ralph Stayer, Chair of the Board and CEO of Johnsonville Sausage LLC, the largest sausage brand in North America, in which Stayer wrote about learning to let his workers lead (Stayer, 1990).

An important starting point for B&J was rebranding its HR department to PPC: 'people, performance and culture'. This was not a superficial exercise to gain employee buy-in but the recognition that 'people, performance and culture' work in tandem and need to be structured accordingly. 'People' emphasizes valuing and empowering employees; 'performance' emphasizes employees taking responsibility and accountability for their behaviours and outputs as a team; 'culture' emphasizes employees understanding the wider organizational objectives and ensuring that B&J's policies, communication, and behaviours are aligned. The outcomes of this rebranding process have been productivity increase by 15%, volume increase by 17%, a higher employee satisfaction rate, and lower staff turnover.

When observing discussions among the senior leadership team, we found frank and open discussions, although there was a reluctance to repeatedly challenge Beak given his role as the founder of the business. Some members also suggested that the structure of the reporting was not always clear, which created some ambiguities around authority, responsibility, and accountability. This catalysed Beak's appointment of two CEOs for the two major divisions of the business (meat; soups and meals), while he was group CEO. He saw this as an interim process before becoming Executive Chair with only one CEO who reports directly to him. At the time of our interviews, he said to us that 'I want CEOs to be CEOs', meaning empowering them to make strategic decisions, having full operational control of the business, and managing performance. Beak said he would be group CEO for a short time before becoming chair: 'My role is to set the vision with the Board, appoint my successors, and get out of the way'.

Eight years on from the original research, he did move to chair, he has restructured and simplified the senior leadership team, and the business is close to meeting its target of becoming a billion-dollar company. When I spoke to Beak in 2022, he told me that B&J have totally disrupted their business model and have moved entirely away from fresh case ready meat and instead to pre-prepared meals, slow cooked meats, and lasagne. They are also working closely with Impossible Foods Inc. in California, which develops plant-based substitutes for meat products. B&J's total production volumes are the same, but growing at more than 15% compared to a 7% decline in fresh meat. In the words of Beak, and borrowing the words of former professional ice hockey player and coach Wayne Gretzky, B&J are now 'skating to where the puck is going to be'.

With the cultural change of people adopting a more vegetarian diet—which poses a threat to B&J—a starting point was a change in the structure of the divisions of the company such as finance, production, investment, and management. While on the surface this may appear mundane and irrelevant to culture, this was important as it meant that each operational line of the business could be accountable to its own targets. In the past, different divisions of the business had operated within silos, which had caused tensions between divisions and meant that these divisions of the business adopted a short-term approach that may have suited them, but did not take a wider strategic view of the needs of B&J. The previous structure also created a top-down targets-based culture that focused on divisional targets and suppressed employee innovation and empowerment. There was a telling parallel identified by the Chief Financial Officer and the Chief Operating Officer of a lack of employee empowerment with behavioural norms from the top trickling down to employee behaviours. They highlighted, for example, that Beak himself interfered with the minutiae of the business, which he personally recognized was a challenge for him to overcome. Because Beak had worked on the front line and built the business from scratch, he was highly respected by employees and managers across B&J, reinforcing the importance of leaders' roles in modelling desired behaviours.

One way of developing employee behaviours was through the creation of a simple set of organizational values, which were referred to as 'The B&J Way'. Within this set of values was a strong overarching commitment to safety, high quality standards, exceeding the expectations of stakeholders, and setting short- and long-term goals that require personal growth and high performance. Employees were asked to commit to these values through their performance and accountability to the team, through their ongoing investment in their personal development. B&J has supported the emphasis on personal development and standards by providing greater management training, a fast-track promotion scheme for consistent high performance, and encouragement of behaviours and performance aligning to the organization's strategy.

Historically, there were tensions between two shift teams on the factory floor: the day shift between 5.30am and 2.30pm and the afternoon shift between 2.30pm and midnight. The culture of the day shift was gung-ho, with line managers choosing the easiest meat lines to run and running as many as possible. This showed at a surface level that performance and yields were high. In contrast, the culture of the afternoon shift was a highly pressured environment because of the immediate need to meet the 3–3.30pm cut-off time when trucks would arrive at the factory to pick up all the meat for delivery to the supermarkets. Given the time-sensitive nature of pick-ups and the limited shelf life of meat products, this meant that both the pressure and responsibility to meet critical deadlines rested on the afternoon shift who were considered as the problem when deadlines were missed, whereas the morning shift was perceived as productive and high performing. Not surprisingly, this created tensions between managers and members of both shift teams, and created perverse behaviours that suited the needs of the individual shifts rather than meeting the overarching strategic objectives of delivering high quality products safely and on time.

Identifying these tensions triggered more effective communication between shifts, and line managers' delivery targets were altered to suit the whole organization rather than the preferences of individual lines. Within these parameters, line managers were empowered to approach the operational challenges of their lines in ways that they saw as appropriate and were encouraged to share these practices with others to learn from successes and setbacks.

The challenges of leadership and culture at B&J have valuable lessons for how to manage reputation threats in other contexts. Working in a large meat factory is a harsh environment: it is cold, in order to preserve the shelf life of the meat; staff are using potentially dangerous tools and machinery to cut meat; they are required to wear a lot of protective equipment; and they are under pressure to meet tight deadlines which are costly for the organization if missed. Creating a positive leadership and cultural environment within this context is not easy, but possible. While this environment might appear distinct, other contexts such as hospital theatres, battlefields, trading floors, and warehouses are just a few of many examples of how different organizational contexts can present similar kinds of leadership and cultural challenges, which if not effectively managed can present escalating threats.

Escalation is an important term because as discussed in Table 8.1 in relation to reputation-identity gaps, small issues can become medium-level problems or large-scale crises if they are left to stagnate and are not effectively managed. An important stakeholder that is relevant to all three examples that I have discussed in this chapter is employees. They are the face of the organization for professional service firms such as management consulting firms when they are interacting with clients, and in the case of the meat industry, like other product-based organizations, they are essential for ensuring productivity.

The positive attitude and commitment of employees is fundamental for every organization. Morally, strategically, and economically, it is logical for organizations to look after their employees because the benefits are great and the costs are catastrophic if they get things wrong.

Throughout the book, I have discussed many ways of engaging employees through purpose, values, engagement, and empowerment. A further important approach, which has become particularly apparent since the onset and aftermath of the coronavirus pandemic, is managing employee wellbeing, which is the focus of the next chapter.

9

Doing Well by Doing Good

Health and wellbeing are essential for organizations. When employees are well, happy, and motivated then they will be engaged and productive. When they are unwell, unhappy, and demotivated then they will be disengaged and unproductive at work. Even more pressingly, unhappy employees at work leads to unhappy relationships outside of work, which has negative consequences for them, their families, friends, and wider society. Hence, notwithstanding the economic benefits, first and foremost organizations have a moral duty to look after their people because it is the right thing to do.

There are also reputation benefits from looking after your employees. As I discussed in Chapter 3, the reputation of organizations within the labour market, which includes potential and existing employees, has moral and productivity outcomes for organizations. It is also something that potential and existing employees care about and is therefore being measured and publicly shared. In this chapter, I outline four distinct examples of understanding doing well by doing good. First, I outline the example of Surfwell, an innovative intervention for Devon and Cornwall Police employees to help promote and support their health and wellbeing, in a context where talking about mental health within the UK police force has historically been stigmatized (Tourky et al., 2021). Second, I look at how executive search firms in Australia managed to navigate the common threat of the global financial crisis of 2007–2008. Third, I look at the leadership practices within the principal kingdoms of Nagaland and how a seemingly brutal society of tattoo-faced warriors and headhunters (not executive search firms!) can paradoxically demonstrate lessons of compassion (Featherstone and Harvey, 2021). Fourth, I explore the influence of Daoist nothingness, which focuses on letting go and empowering others rather than instrumental goals and coerciveness, in Chinese leadership practices among small and medium enterprises

Reputations at Stake. William S. Harvey, Oxford University Press. © William S. Harvey (2023).
DOI: 10.1093/oso/9780192886521.003.0009

(SMEs) in Shanghai. These four different illustrations of commitment to the wellbeing of employees, members of the community, and wider stakeholders highlight that there are various ways to support others that are appropriate to the setting.

Surfwell: Health and Wellbeing Within Devon and Cornwall Police

Surfwell is a health intervention that uses the experience of surfing for recreational purposes to promote workplace mental health. It focuses on action-centred therapy, peer support, and group therapy and is a response to a growing mental health crisis within UK emergency services—for example, the 47% increase in police sickness attributed to mental health compared to the previous five years between 2012 and 2017 (Police Fire Arms Association, 2017). Despite a concerted effort through high-profile campaigns to destigmatize mental health across the emergency services, stigma continues to be a barrier for emergency services workers to seek support (Kings College London, 2020).

Surfwell was introduced to address the persistence of stigma and the need for relevant support through a peer-based approach to managing mental health (Tourky et al., 2021) conceived by two Devon and Cornwall police sergeants, Sam Davies and James Mallows (see Diagram 9.1), after an officer they were supervising was left traumatized by an attack and for whom other clinical treatments were ineffective.

Diagram 9.1 Surfwell

The study specifically focused on the impact of Surfwell on individual wellbeing and mental health as well as on the organizational outcomes for Devon and Cornwall Police. The scheme allows police officers facing mental health and wellbeing issues to spend a day in a challenging but safe environment learning to surf under the guidance of expert facilitators who themselves are serving police officers. The combination of trusted colleagues, a supportive peer group, cold water, natural surroundings, and learning a new skill provide a safe and enjoyable environment for participants to share their emotions, feelings, and experiences. Because it is voluntary and officers can self-refer, this removes the perceived stigma of having to seek help through an occupational health expert, although they can be referred through this route as well. Participants are encouraged to stay in touch with their peers and some choose to join the police surf club as a hobby and mechanism to manage stress when it arises.

Data were collected in 2019 and 2020 from twenty officers who had been involved in the Surfwell programme because they had experienced mild or moderate mental health difficulties (Tourky et al., 2021). Eight middle and senior members of Devon and Cornwall Police were interviewed, including superintendents and chief inspectors as well as the three sergeants running Surfwell, to gauge their experiences of the programme from the perspective of leaders and managers having to navigate the different perceptions and operational realities of Surfwell. The experiences of six females and fourteen males, aged between 36 and 59, were analysed. Data were collected through pre- and post-session surveys, interviews, and focus groups.

How Does Doing Good Make an Organization Do Well?

Perhaps unsurprisingly, the doing good in this initiative led to positive outcomes: benefits for both participating police officers as well as for Devon and Cornwall Police were reported.

At the individual level, we found statistically significant improvements for individuals: feeling optimistic about the future, feeling useful, feeling relaxed, and feeling close to others. In the words of one female participant, 'I've literally gone from driving home after every shift upset to coming here and feeling more energetic ... They [Surfwell facilitators] just make you feel so special'. There were some immediate personal gains from participants, including a positive change in mood, a sense of achievement, improved confidence, acceptance of having mental health issues, and renewed motivation. 'I'm probably in the worst headspace I've ever been in and I pretty much spent all of Monday crying and so to be here today smiling, is a complete leap ... I feel energetic. I feel happy. Like there's this buzz when you come out'. After the buzz of the initial experience had worn off, researchers later followed up with participants and it was evident that there were more sustained gains, including personal gains in their growth in resilience, hope, optimism, and self-efficacy. 'It just gave me a sense of being somebody rather than I'm plodding along every day, getting on, not really getting any answers to my problems and my issues but that I was actually somebody that was worth it'.

At the organizational level, we found statistically significant improvements for the organization around feelings of satisfaction, enjoying discussing Devon and Cornwall Police with people outside the force, feeling strong and vigorous on the job, feeling enthusiastic about the job, and feeling interested in the job. 'Just knowing there is the group out there that are looking out for me makes me feel much better towards the organization so more invested in making sure I am keeping myself well and turning up and doing my best', said one male participant. Another participant was candid in how he had a lot of mental health challenges that meant that the wrong approach from the organization could easily have forced him to go off sick, which in turn would create logistical and financial challenges for Devon and Cornwall Police: 'I've got a lot of things on my mind right now that are not related to work ... and I know that if I don't have some way to deal with those issues then I'd be off sick quite easily ... but by doing something like this it keeps you balanced. The organization will gain massively because I'll be at work as opposed to having to back fill me for the next six months'. Another participant said, 'I couldn't cope with everything so I was about to hand in my notice and just say "I don't want to do this anymore". I love my job, but I was just struggling at that time and I can wholeheartedly say the only reason I didn't leave the police was because of Surfwell, because of the support I found from the facilitators and peers, 100% that's why I didn't leave the job'. Long-term reputation benefits for Devon and Cornwall Police can be seen because of Surfwell, including positive perceptions around the support it provides to people with mental health and wellbeing challenges, reductions in staff absenteeism, and higher levels of staff retention.

The response of senior leaders and middle managers was extremely positive in terms of the innovation and outcomes of Surfwell. However, two tensions continued to be a challenge. First, ongoing public sector cutbacks meant managers responsible for delivering front-line services (such as running a police station) found it difficult to cover staff absences for Surfwell even though they recognized the individual and organizational benefits of the intervention. This created some tension and challenges for those officers who were covering staff participating in the scheme. Second, while senior leaders were very supportive of increasing the health and wellbeing support for their staff, given the distinctiveness of Surfwell they were concerned that the potential headline of 'tax payers funding the police to take the day off surfing', however misconstrued, was a very real perceived reputation threat to both Surfwell and Devon and Cornwall Police.

In short, in the early stages of its development Surfwell has had major immediate and sustained health and wellbeing benefits for participants as well as reputation benefits for Devon and Cornwall Police. That said, the operational, financial, and perceptual (internal and external) challenges mean that even though this is a positive initiative, there are still significant reputation risks to navigate.

Pivoting During a Global Financial Crisis in Executive Recruitment

The second example involves research that I conducted with my colleagues Jon Beaverstock and Hongqin Li on executive search firms in Australia, and how these firms managed the common threat of the global financial crisis of 2007–2008 (Harvey et al., 2019). This was a highly challenging time for all organizations, including executive search firms, whose bread and butter was searching and attracting top candidates for specific roles for their clients at a time when firms were not hiring. The global financial crisis, like Brexit and the coronavirus pandemic, are examples of common threats that are faced by multiple sectors. At the time of the research, executive search firms had faced few common threats because of the powerful structural position of partners who were well connected with influential clients in elite labour markets in a confidential and discrete sector (Garrison Jenn, 2005). The Australian economy had at the time also experienced many consecutive decades of growth, largely owing to the booming resources sector that created significant demand from executive search firms to place talent.

The global financial crisis presented three particular threats for the executive search sector.

1. Major reduction in demand from clients to place talent.
2. Desperate tactics from a few 'cowboys' in the sector, some disquiet around the trustworthiness of executive search.
3. Incumbents being threatened by new online search offerings which questioned the value of existing executive search firms.

In short, the macro-economic crisis triggered challenges in relation to demand, status, and value within the sector. I would classify this as large in Table 8.1 because these threats meant that many executive search firms failed. Not surprisingly, the initial response to these threats was to reduce the number of partners and consultants related to search work, but more surprisingly some firms opened offices up to offer new services.

During the interviews with executive firm partners, we asked what they were doing to respond to the common threats. We found there were broadly three types of responses that different firms were taking that we refer to as functional, symbolic, and individual strategies.

Functional strategies involve firms recognizing that their business model is under threat and that survival depends on a fundamentally different approach. For example, some firms started offering leadership development services and leadership assessment tools, which was considered credible given their knowledge of engagement with leaders as part of their search business.

With symbolic strategies, we found that firms focused on highlighting their elite status, for example the location of their offices, the clients that they had worked for, and the qualifications of their professionals. However, we found a divided approach to highlighting symbolic capital, with some firms able to move upstream and others forced to move downstream. Upstream included focusing on lower-volume and higher-level positions such as chief executives, chairs, and directors, as well as allied services such as succession planning and leadership assessment. Downstream included focusing on higher-volume and middle-level management positions where there was more demand for search work, but the potential risk of losing business in the long-term for senior-level appointments.

With individual strategies, we found a lot of evidence of partners doubling down in their efforts to connect with clients to win new and retain existing work. Several partners mentioned the importance of managing their rolodex[1] and reminding clients of the value they provide. This impression management approach was a way to keep their firm in the minds of their clients and as a soft way of sustaining its reputation. Partners also reached out to their pool of candidates, trying to maintain personal relationships and gauging how their business was going. They intended to fend off new competitors entering the field in the future. In the words of one partner, 'brand gets you to the table', so maintaining that brand even when there was limited work was a strategy to ensure they were shortlisted for tenders when new work started to return.

Functional strategies, such as diversifying services, was something new for executive search firms as they found themselves pivoting into areas that they had not delivered before. In contrast, symbolic strategies (such as impression management techniques) and individual strategies (such as strategic networking) were areas that firms had historically engaged with in a passive way but were now pursuing during the crisis in a much more proactive, strategic, and professional manner. Although individual executive search firms adopted some or a combination of functional, symbolic, and individual strategies similar to their competitors, we found there are wider lessons to be learned from the

---

[1] A rolodex is a brand name for a small circular file of business cards that sits on a desk.

English idiom 'keeping up with the Joneses' as a way of understanding how organizations can manage their reputations in response to common threats. In this case, 'the Joneses' refers to competitors.

The first lesson is to move away from the Joneses, which implies offering a very different set of activities to previous ones so they can no longer be compared to the same set of competitors. In our cases, some firms were offering new services upstream for senior leaders, whereas other firms were occupying search services downstream, in both cases altering who they were competing with.

The second lesson is networking more than the Joneses, which describes greater proactivity in connecting with different stakeholders to informally highlight the value of their work. From our research, this entailed partners of executive search firms reaching out to their clients and candidates even when it was not apparent that there was an immediate business opportunity. In fact, connecting with clients and candidates more broadly appeared to trigger wider conversations and gain broader support around their circumstances than more direct transactional conversations.

The third lesson involves fencing out the Joneses, which describes firms showing how they are distinctive from the poor behaviour of their competitors. Several interviewees expressed their frustration with a small number of 'cowboys', individuals who had quickly set up their own business and were winning a lot of work but who were not managing their relations with clients and candidates—thus undermining the reputation of the sector. Incumbents therefore found themselves working hard to signal the quality of their own working practices and to ostracize the practices of others to avoid compromising their own reputation as well as the reputation of the sector. While on the surface this may seem like an isolated context, it is likely to become more common; for example a few rogue investment bankers undermining wider perceptions of the sector, or energy companies greenwashing customers with talk about their commitment to the environment when other energy companies are trying to show activists and investors that they are genuinely committed to decarbonizing.

In summary, functional, symbolic, and individual strategies combined with moving away from the Joneses, networking more than the Joneses,

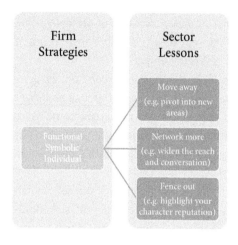

Diagram 9.2 Managing Reputation in Response to Common Threats

and fencing out the Joneses are some approaches organizations can adopt to manage their reputation in response to common threats (see Diagram 9.2).

The Konyaks of Nagaland: Compassion Among Headhunters

In 2021, I worked with Justin Featherstone on an ethnographic project based on his experience of living with the Konyak ethnic group in the Mon district of Nagaland (Featherstone and Harvey, 2021). During this time, he spoke extensively to thirteen tattoo-faced warriors, four women who can recollect the headhunting times, and nineteen members of the community from different age groups. We were interested in the paradox of tough and kind forms of leadership, drawing on the experience of the last surviving tattoo-faced warriors. For centuries and up until the 1950s, the villages of the principal Konyak kingdoms in Nagaland had raided each other and beheaded men, women, and children as part of ritualized hostilities. With origins in fertility and harvests, this practice was predominantly an expression of power, which was believed to be held in the human skull.

Headhunting raids typically involved between thirty to forty warriors over one or two nights' march away. Ambushes would take place at first light and one warrior would be responsible for shooting the target with a musket made by the tribe, while another would decapitate the victim with his dao, an axe-like implement. There was no distinction between combatants and non-combatants, and heads were taken from men, women, and children. On the surface, this conjures-up a brutal regime and negative forms of autocratic leadership which involve the exertion of control over others.

Surprisingly, the tough leadership regime of the Konyaks was under-pinned by a leadership ethos that emphasized kindness. The Konyak's view of kindness is that it should exist alongside toughness. It was clear that kindness reflected the interactions between three generations, from tattoo-faced warriors to children. Today, the use of tattooing to mark major events in the lives of Konyak men and women has disappeared because of its association with headhunting. Featherstone (2022) found that kindness was a central part of Konyak culture, but should not be confused with taking the easy path: kind leaders should take responsibility for doing the right thing which may require being tough. He concluded that it was not so much whether the Konyaks were tough or kind, but that they developed toughness through kindness. This was as true for Anghs (hereditary kings) as it was for council members, teachers, and parents among the Konyaks.

Notwithstanding an underpinning of kindness, toughness remains a regular activity for Konyaks today. For example, boys particularly are encouraged to catch and slaughter wild buffalo in the surrounding forests to display strength and courage among their peers. Young children are encouraged to trap rats and hunt game from a very young age. Homes are decorated with buffalo and cattle skulls as well as tigers, bears, and wild cats. While some of this is a legacy of colonial rule with the encouragement of wild animal displays rather than human displays, there remains an emphasis on toughness.

Surprisingly, kindness has greater weighting than strength and resilience among the Konyaks today (Featherstone and Harvey, 2021). For instance, it is the Angh's responsibility to safeguard the wellbeing of his people. There is also a strong sense of responsibility within the community to support those in need, from fostering an orphan to sharing rice and crops with others following a poor harvest, or providing labour for the fields for families who have been affected by illness or death. When someone dies, the community comes together to mourn with the grieving family, each rotating to support the family over a twenty-four-hour period. While authority is clear and respected, decisions are usually made collaboratively with families able to represent their views.

Leaders are expected to listen purposefully to the different voices within their community. Women now occupy leadership positions within religious and educational establishments. They can—though this has yet to materialize—become members of the Village Council; this illustrates that progression is still needed, although our interviewees said that they were on the cusp of change. The combination of tough and kind leadership seemed to resonate with Goffee and Jones' (2000) notion of tough empathy, which can be found in other martial communities. For example, the Royal Military Academy Sandhurst, which trains officers for the British Army, follows the motto 'Serve to Lead'.

An obvious question is how toughness and kindness can coexist? One answer from the Konyaks is through the concept of matkapu, which crudely translates as 'standing for the truth of things'. This requires leaders to reflect on the consequences of their actions, including what this may mean for others within the community as well as a broader set of groups (Bower and Paine, 2017). This has enabled a balance between those competing forces of toughness and kindness (see Diagram 9.3).

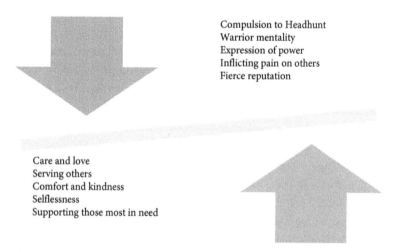

Compulsion to Headhunt
Warrior mentality
Expression of power
Inflicting pain on others
Fierce reputation

Care and love
Serving others
Comfort and kindness
Selflessness
Supporting those most in need

Diagram 9.3 Balancing Toughness and Kindness

While the brutality of headhunting alongside compassion and care is difficult to apply in other contexts, this extreme case does illustrate the importance of organizational kindness to help overcome toughness. In a business context, the term cut-throat refers to competing in a powerful and unfair way without considering the harm caused on others. Perhaps kindness alongside toughness helps over time to dilute toxic cultures.

Daoist Nothingness: SME Leaders in China

The final example of doing well by doing good draws on the example of SME leaders in China. Daoism emphasizes the importance of non-action, for example taking a more relaxed approach to setting goals, spontaneously forging connections rather than doing this instrumentally, and letting reputation building occur in unintended ways. Drawing on work with my colleagues Hongqin Li, Oswald Jones, and JieYang (Li et al., 2021), we interviewed twelve Chinese leaders who were founders of fast growing SMEs within the logistics industry in Shanghai as well as five senior external leaders. This is an important sector that at the time of the fieldwork was valued at approximately $37 trillion across China (Chyxx, 2019), with 90% of logistics businesses in Shanghai being comprised of SMEs. We found strong evidence for Daoist nothingness. There is a temptation to impose our own cultural lenses onto other business contexts, but we found that Daoism was important for Chinese leaders. Daoism is a philosophical foundation that differentiates Chinese leadership from Western concepts (Chan, 1970). Rather than an instrumental approach to achieving goals such as building reputation, we found that leaders adopted a letting-go approach (Wenning, 2011).

Under the Daoist approach, we found that leaders let the reputation of their businesses evolve locally in different ways under the banner of locating, openness, and low profile. Locating describes how leaders tried to understand and then respond to the needs of different groups. This ranged from employees who needed mentoring or support with accommodation to suppliers who had supported them at important stages of the business. Importantly, rather than supporting these people with the motivation to gain some form of return (e.g. interest on a loan or reciprocal payment for a service), the SME leaders described their spontaneous response. These leaders were not educated in management and leadership, and they described how they sought to navigate their way through these challenges spontaneously by picking up on cues. One of the leaders, Qing, said he was guided by 'putting himself in the shoes of frontline workers' and asking 'Does the firm satisfy my needs?' and subsequently addressing issues that he had uncovered.

With openness, leaders were candid that they took a laissez-faire approach given they did not have prior training or support in leadership. In these instances, these leaders explained how they followed their intuition or went with the flow. This was considered very important in their context because the business environment in China was rapidly growing and changing. One leader, Xue, attempted to provide his employees with an 'open space', which meant flexibility, empowerment, and delegation that contributed to them feeling positive about the organization. He explained how this approach was learned from prior mistakes with two previous start-ups when he was overly structured and detail-orientated, which was less effective at empowering and engaging his staff.

We found that SME leaders preferred to adopt a low-profile approach. This contrasts with the emphasis on celebrity leaders and prominence in Western contexts (Hayward et al., 2004; Lange et al., 2011; Graffin et al., 2013), particularly in an era of social media, where seemingly greater notoriety is something that leaders and organizations strive for. Our sample of SME leaders tended to work with their employees to identify roles and opportunities that were suited to them, rather than prescribed through narrow and arbitrary job descriptions. Often such conversations would occur in informal settings such as over lunch, and frequently they stated how they were surprised that they would learn things about communication and leadership from their employees that they had not considered.

SME leaders also reflected on building the wider reputation of their business through attention generation, uncertainty reduction, and evaluation. Indirect attention generation can be a valuable way to widen reputation building. For example, one of our participants, Chang, described when he spontaneously invited one of his customers to lunch. There was no agenda and it was a spur of the moment decision. Initially, the customer was quite embarrassed to accept, but Chang invited the customer to understand his needs better. When we spoke to the customer he reflected on how that touched him because all of his interactions with others were transactional. This led to the customer calling Chang later as he wanted to reciprocate the gesture by offering further business, which triggered a specialist sub-category of logistics at the very early stages that has subsequently led to significant growth. Another example was when Ge was mentoring a leader with a mooncake business who had no reputation in the market and found himself having to set his price point low. Ge suggested ways for his mentee to make his business distinctive such as offering mini mooncakes, which the mentee had a good feeling about and pursued. When we spoke to the mentee, he said that 80% of the mini mooncakes in Shanghai are now provided by his company. The lesson from these examples is that doing good in a non-instrumental way can have unintended positive outcomes both for oneself and for others.

SME leaders also reduced uncertainty for themselves and others by doing good. When we interviewed Jie, we discussed with him how he managed to build a successful logistics company in a saturated market when he had limited education and networks and came from the countryside of an isolated province. His response was that being a good leader and a decent person to others had helped him weather the storms during difficult times. For example, he explained that on several occasions when the business had cashflow problems others had stepped in to support him. Individuals ranged from senior managers, board members, and customers. We cross-checked this story with a senior member of the Shanghai Logistics Committee who said that he had known Jie for nearly ten years and that he had built a strong reputation in the sector. He explained how this had encouraged him to help Jie through introductions to other Board members to help his business. The moral of this example is that running a good business alongside being a good person can be important for helping leaders to manage crises through securing various forms of support from internal and external stakeholders.

We found that evaluation of a leader's behaviour can lead to positive unintended outcomes. Qiang, for example, explained how he managed to grow his business from £23,000 to £200,000, but struggled to grow it further without a large injection of capital. To his surprise, the source of that capital ended up coming from the landlord from whom he leased his office, who was impressed with his reliability and ethical business conduct. Qiang explained that he did not expect this level of investment from his business landlord and it was not the reason why he behaved in the way he did; nevertheless the financial support was vital in helping his business to rapidly double in size.

Another example was the decision of leaders in their conduct to focus on long-term sustainable growth rather than opportunistic short-term growth. Ying described how there were a lot of cowboys in his sector who were fixated on immediate financial returns, but highly dubious in terms of their ethical conduct. However, he said that a high level of integrity was not at odds with but rather fundamental to the long-term growth of the business. He gave the example of a customer who had recently become aware of several logistic suppliers who were acting unethically, which compromised their trust and led to the cancellation of their contracts. Ying was concerned that there could be a contagion effect and that this malpractice could impact on the reputation of his firm. However, the perceived contrast of his firm's conduct with those of the cowboys in fact led to Ying's firm receiving these contracts. Ying said that this reinforced to him how important his behaviours were and led to him starting a process of further strengthening the moral values within his organization, both among employees and in recognition of how they can impact on external perceptions.

In summary, this fourth example of SME leaders in the Shanghai logistics sector shows that some degree of non-action is important. Significantly, this is not the same as doing nothing because what underpinned all the examples was a clear purpose to do good without expecting some kind of return, akin to Adam Grant's (2013) notion of *Give and Take*. This combination of spontaneous support for others, a strong ethical code of conduct, and the relaxation of pre-determined intentions is distinct from impressions of hierarchical, authoritarian, and directive forms of leadership (Farh and Cheng, 2000; Chen et al., 2017). It also provides a different lens to well-known Western forms of leadership such as authentic, transformational, and responsible leadership, among others (Burns, 1978; Avolio and Gardner, 2005; Maak et al.,

2016). The examples also show how for many organizations there is an important relationship between the leader's conduct and reputation and how the wider organization is perceived. This is clearly important for eponymous, family, and small firms where founders and CEOs are often the driving force behind the prominence and growth of the organization. However, the lessons reach further because leaders of prominent organizations such as large political parties, supranational organizations, corporations, private firms, and charities receive a large volume of attention through mass media, social media, and other third parties, meaning their individual conduct can have far-reaching consequences for their organizations in terms of their reputation.

This chapter has highlighted through four examples how doing good can look quite different in various contexts. In all four cases there is a link between individual, organizational, and societal levels: the behaviours and actions of individuals, particularly leaders, have wider implications on the organization and society. It is also worth reiterating that what can sometimes seem alien or even brutal on the surface, may surprisingly have valuable lessons of leadership and ethical conduct that we can learn from in other contexts. From lessons of ethical conduct and doing good, it would be remiss of me to neglect the darker side of this shiny coin. From here we move to the growing threat of professional misconduct.

10

The Growing Threat of Professional Misconduct

The premise of this book, *Reputations at Stake*, focuses on the multiple challenges related to reputation. I have discussed in previous chapters the different kinds of threats that organizations face, ranging from climate change and the coronavirus pandemic to the single actions of organizations, leaders, and employees. There is mounting evidence that professional misconduct is growing considering rising pressures related to the coronavirus pandemic. For example, the UK's Department for Business, Energy and Industrial Strategy (BEIS) estimates that the Bounce Back Loan Scheme, which was introduced until the end of March 2021 to help small businesses access finance more quickly during the coronavirus pandemic, could cost the taxpayer £27 billion in fraud or credit losses (UK Parliament, 2021). Although the figures are stark, they are not surprising given that governments, businesses, leaders, employees, families, and societies have faced health, economic, and social pressures that many have not experienced in their lifetimes. This is showing through a deterioration in mental health across the world (Abbott, 2021) and places a strain on all of us in terms of our decision-making.

Alongside the human response to the pandemic increasing the risk profile of people committing professional misconduct, there are also rapidly changing technological shifts and work patterns where individual and organizational behaviours are outpacing regulatory oversight. Technological examples include growing applications of artificial intelligence, the threat of synthesized media (also known as deep fakes), cryptocurrencies, non-fungible tokens (NFTs), and the blurring of the real world and the virtual world through augmented reality (AR), virtual reality (VR), and metaverse platforms. Work examples include remote

Reputations at Stake. William S. Harvey, Oxford University Press. © William S. Harvey (2023).
DOI: 10.1093/oso/9780192886521.003.0010

working and new models of working, which are further blurring the boundaries between work, home, and social time. The growing application of individual data for commercial and other purposes, ranging from technology, supermarkets, banks, music, and sports firms holding large volumes of data, also presents risks that the commercialization of individual data is at odds with current legal expectations. This remains a risk despite legislation such as the general data protection regulation (GDPR), which is a regulation in EU law on data protection and privacy in the European Union and the European Economic Area.

An uncomfortable truth is that the wrong mixture of environmental context, organizational culture, and individual circumstances means there is a risk that we could all succumb to professional misconduct. This is not an easy message to accept because many of us would like to think that being dismissed from a job or receiving a prison sentence is very far removed from our own reality. However, in this chapter I bring a reality check to this myth, drawing on a unique research project conducted with my colleague Navdeep Arora on white-collar inmates in a United States Federal Prison. As we explain elsewhere (Harvey and Arora, 2021), this was a very challenging context for both of us as student and supervisor; however the rich data that we collected from inmates and prison officers provides a novel lens for understanding professional misconduct. In particular, through speaking to people who were reflecting on their past actions in prison, we draw out important lessons about what causes people to act in a way that leads to a dramatic loss of reputation.

Background on the Prison Project

In July 2016, I was approached by Navdeep Arora about a potential PhD project on building reputation within digital start-ups. What we ended up with was a project on reputation damage and repairing reputation owing to Navdeep's own eighteen-month sentencing for wire fraud in March 2018. During the early stages of the prison sentence, we were having one of our regular fifteen-minute telephone calls, which was the time limit set by the prison service. Navdeep mentioned how there were many other well-educated and previously successful businesspeople who were also serving prison sentences for white-collar crime. This sparked two core questions in my mind: first, what causes people to commit professional misconduct from the perspective of those who have been convicted of such crimes? Second, what can we learn from those who have catastrophically damaged their reputation about how people can repair their identity, reputation, and lives? These two themes form the basis of the next two chapters. Once we had agreed the scope of the project and had received ethical approval, we started the process of Navdeep speaking to the inmates.

A question I have commonly been asked is how do I know whether the responses of inmates provide us with genuine insights. My response to this is twofold. First, we had exceptional access to interviewing inmates and conducting focus groups with them in the prison when they were spending large amounts of time reflecting on their past actions and contemplating their future. In addition to the formal data collection during interviews and focus groups, there were many informal discussions during meal and break times where our participants would candidly and generously share their experience. Second, Navdeep led all these conversations and because he was a peer, living and breathing a similar challenging experience as others, there was not the same risk of these participants putting on a show for an external interviewer. Indeed, over time and as trust was built, interviewees shared very personal details, often outpouring their emotions as they shared their stories. This is significant because they had little to prove or gain from projecting a false impression of their past. Given the difficulty of accessing inmates while they are in prison and because we benefitted from an insider rather than an outsider conducting the research, this gave us confidence in both the veracity and novelty of the data.

We collected data for sixteen months in 2018 and 2019 and conducted interviews with seventy inmates on at least two occasions and sometimes three if they had not already left the prison. Each interview lasted between one and three hours. We also conducted twenty focus groups with between six to ten participants to help us probe on issues that had emerged from the interviews. The participants that were included in our sample had all been incarcerated for white-collar crimes. As the prison was single sex, all participants were male. The age of participants at the time of the fieldwork ranged from 27 to 71, with the median age being 47 years. Participants came from a wide range of professional backgrounds and included CEOs, investment and fund managers, management consultants, medical doctors, real estate developers, accountants, entrepreneurs, and public sector leaders. Finally, we were able to speak to the education officers at the prison who had witnessed many hundreds of white-collar inmates come and go. They were also well placed to address our two core questions that we will look at in this chapter and the next.

What Causes People to Commit Professional Misconduct?

Professional misconduct can be understood as a continuum of incidences and actions that range from illegal behaviour (that is against the law), to unprofessional behaviour (that breaches a professional code of conduct), to unethical behaviour (that is at odds with societal expectations) (Gabbionetta et al., 2019). The boundaries between what is right and wrong can often be quite grey because the actions of some people and their organizations are ahead of regulation. The role of social media platforms in overseeing individual behaviour, the tax contributions of large technology firms, or the investment patterns in cryptocurrencies are just three examples of how public opinion, regulation, and the rule of law are struggling to keep apace with current practices. Because the boundaries between right and wrong are both shifting and complex, this creates an environment for people and organizations to sleepwalk into professional misconduct (Muzio et al., 2016).

It is both tempting and convenient to assume that professional misconduct is a function of one 'bad apple', namely a rogue individual. This is easier for organizations to explain to their stakeholders because by severing their ties with the individual the implication is that they have no culpability, which is the advice that their legal and public relations advisors would give. It is also the typical narrative that we read in news bulletins, newspaper headlines, and online newsfeeds. However, extending the 'bad apples' metaphor, there are also 'bad barrels' and 'bad cellars' to consider (Muzio et al., 2016). By bad barrels, I refer to weak cultures,

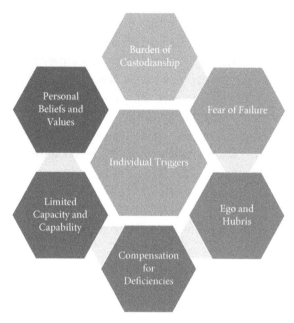

Diagram 10.1 Individual Triggers of Professional
Misconduct

governance, structures, and practices within organizations. For example,
if there is a toxic culture or perverse incentives that encourage particular outcomes, then it is not surprising that individuals and teams will
behave in a particular way (Covaleski et al., 1998). The demise of Enron
Corporation in the US in 2001 has commonly been explained by toxic
leadership and workplace culture, which eroded the organization's management control and governance systems (Free and Macintosh, 2008).
The collapse of Kids Company in the UK is another example of a failed
organization; in this case weak governance was blamed, with trustees
being too slow to respond to the charity's risky operating model (Charity
Commission, 2022). Bad cellars relate to the wider geopolitical, jurisdic-
tional, and ecological environment in which organizations operate and
individuals reside. For example, a political, legal, industry, and regulatory regime will lend itself to norms of behaviour that may be common
in one region but rare in another.

We found that the combination of individual, organizational, and environmental factors explains why people commit professional misconduct. When analysing and coding our data, we found there were six interconnected triggers at the individual level that explain why people committed professional misconduct. These are summarized in Diagram 10.1, which highlights that they operate collectively rather than in isolation.

Individual Triggers

Burden of custodianship describes the feeling among inmates that they had a responsibility to meet the needs of a wider set of stakeholders. Many people described their feeling of pressure to meet the demands of their stakeholders. As they recognized, this feeling was construed by themselves rather than a reflection of what these stakeholders expected. One community leader, for example, described his feeling of responsibility:

> With thirty-five employees on our payroll, we were also responsible for their families, so more than 100 people at least. As the construction market tanked, so did our revenue from construction supplies. We could not make payroll, so I moved money from employee benefit and retirement accounts to payroll. It was a short-term fix and we hoped that the business would pick back up within a year. It took much longer and then it was too late.

However flawed the logic, the decision of moving employee benefits to payroll came from a position of this leader wanting to support his employees. Tragically and ironically, this approach failed and had the opposite effect to its intent.

Fear of failure occurred when people were focused on self-preservation. Part of this was the fear that they risked losing their reputation and therefore would take proactive steps to preserve it. Again, this was ironic because the very steps that they took to preserve their reputations were the cause of their demise. One of our participants who was a founder of an organization explains that, at the time of his actions, he did not appreciate who the victims might have been. Instead, his focus was on preserving the reputation of his organization and its wider stakeholders, which as he explains was the reason for his fall from grace:

> I was told that there were many victims of my crime, but I didn't know any. My intent was to protect the reputation of my company and my partners. They counted on me—as the founder. The only people that got hurt were my family. My desire to save my reputation became my nemesis.

Ego and hubris are well-known explanations for professional misconduct, examples of which date as far back as Aristotle. Shakespeare's work is full of tragic heroes battling their own egos and pride, but more recently the concept has been popularized by Oliver Stone's 1987 film *Wall Street* as well as by Martin Scorsese's 2013 film *The Wolf of Wall Street*, which was based on the memoir by John Belfort. Pride is the ultimate downfall of the tragic hero. Through ego and hubris, those who gain a thrill from risk-taking and take opportunities often benefit and fail based on their timing.

Another characteristic among participants was a perception that they were invincible: 'I was excelling at a powerful and influential blue-chip investment firm', said one investor, 'Everyone wanted us and listened to what we had to say. Nothing wrong could ever happen to us'. Another explained that risk-taking was an important part of his business that was necessary to be successful:

> In the venture investing business, there are no hard lines, just soft ones that we had learned to blow away. If you are not willing to take risks, you cannot be successful in our business. We were problem solvers and aggressive risk takers who always found a way.

What is telling from both quotations is that while there is a recognition of the benefits of being the centre of attention and taking risks, there was no acknowledgment of the downside.

Compensation for deficiencies showed itself in many guises. Many participants shared that they had difficult personal circumstances including children committing suicide, spouses dying of cancer, physical impairment, and divorce, as well as alcohol, drug, and gambling addictions. These circumstances sometimes inflated the aspirations of individuals and contributed to them setting themselves warped goals. One participant shared how he grew up wanting to show his family members what he could achieve:

> I ... grew up wanting to show my parents and siblings what I could achieve. When I joined the real estate firm, the pressure to perform even got higher. The bar I set for myself was so much above what was expected of me but I didn't realise that till the damage was done. I pushed myself to do things no one expected or wanted me to do.

Limited capacity and capability explains the difficulties that individuals found themselves in. Often they were operating in grey areas; for instance, one accountant talked about the liminal space between tax evasion and tax avoidance, and a doctor explained his predicament of prescribing opioids within the law of one US state, but breaching Federal law:

> I had agreed with my partners that if something went wrong, I would be the 'fall guy'. The likelihood of anything going wrong was minimal as we had checked and double-checked with our lawyers. So I transferred funds between accounts, and we were told that we had broken a law. I cannot really complain because we did it with our eyes wide open.

Personal beliefs and values describes a small group of people who fell into three categories. First, they denied they had done any wrong and were still coming to terms with what had happened to them. Second, they argued that there was a large group of others within their organization or in the sector who were acting in a similar way, and they were the unlucky ones who were scapegoated. Third, they claimed no harm, no foul, meaning they had made mistakes but had not come to terms with the damage that their actions had caused to others. One entrepreneur said that part of selling a story to potential investors was to inflate the truth to help ensure funding. He claimed that many other organizations were doing the same and ended up being successful, whereas he was caught out and has suffered the consequences:

Start-ups have to be able to tell a compelling story, and you make things up as you go about your capabilities, customers who want to buy your products, and sales pipeline. Otherwise, it is very difficult to get funded. I can point you to twenty successful companies that followed that exact route to get funded. They succeeded and it never came out. We didn't and got caught.

The six individual triggers do not operate in isolation to explain professional misconduct, but rather operate alongside other triggers. For example, when we coded for different triggers, we found that 24% of participants mentioned two triggers, 53% mentioned three triggers, and 14% mentioned four or five triggers as their reasons for committing professional misconduct. The quotations above hint at factors beyond the individual level explaining why participants committed professional misconduct. Another layer of explanation is activity that occurs within the organization.

Organizational Context

The context of the organization also helped explain why people committed professional misconduct. We did not find that participants were looking to shirk their own responsibility for their actions and shift the blame onto others. However, they were reflecting on and rationalizing where their behaviour stemmed from. There were four aspects to the organizational context that were raised: *culture, governance, structure, and practices*.

Within the *culture* of the organization, participants were clear that there were often expectations from their employers or clients around outcome. As one accountant stated, 'It was all about finding new ways to save on taxes for our clients. That is how we brought in more clients and more business. It was less about our responsibility as lawyers'. This example is particularly relevant given the mounting levels of public scrutiny around the unfairness of tax contributions by many global organizations and high-net-worth individuals.

Governance was another factor that was raised by participants. One participant stated that 'It was all about winning new proposals and booking more fees' and increasing revenue, but that 'No one ever even mentioned impact for our clients and if our clients felt we had success-fully delivered what they were looking for'. There was no stepping back and reflecting on whether the organization had provided a good service to its clients.

Structure was another factor that explained the pressures participants felt from the perspective of the organizational context. One interviewee explained that a large restructuring exercise meant removing large layers of support and control: 'Two rounds of cost reduction resulted in slash-ing one entire layer of the organisation and almost doubling the spans of controls', while 'Sales targets increased at the same time, while we lost most of the sales support staff'. This coupling of less support and greater expectations increased his feeling of pressure.

Another participant said that targets were set every year to underwrite more business at the end of the year, which everyone knew might impact claims in twelve to twenty-four months because the business was taking on as much risk as possible, and yet this was still part of the annual target setting. This kind of exercise placed mounting pressure on the business and encouraged an unsustainable approach to risk-taking.

Many participants explained that there was an underlying acceptance of questionable ethical *practices* so long as the business was performing well and no one was asking any questions. As one participant explained, 'The only time anyone ever questioned me about my approach and the process was when things went bad or we did not meet our numbers. If numbers were good or no bombs had gone off, no one cared about how we got there'.

Another interviewee said: 'My partners and I knew there was a large risk in what we were planning and that we were pushing the bound-aries'. However, they relied on their lawyers to advise them. 'We had always counted on our General Counsel and outside lawyers to cover us. They assured us that we were protected, and we thought the risks were worth taking given the benefits for the firm'. Again, when weighing up the excitement of a business opportunity alongside the legal risk, the business opportunity came through stronger, but was the cause of the individual's downfall.

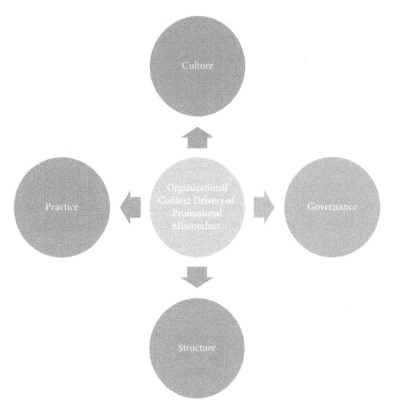

Diagram 10.2 Organizational Context Drivers of Professional Misconduct

Environmental Milieu

Finally, participants also suggested there were three wider environmental factors that explained their professional misconduct.

1. Participants across multiple sectors said that they and their colleagues struggled to keep apace with changes. As I allude to above, often growing regulatory expectations operated alongside staff cuts within the organization and higher levels of targets. As one medical doctor explains, 'The government had launched a national campaign on pain management and encouraged new research

and treatment protocols. I was a well-acclaimed medical doctor and researcher in the space and was doing my duty by treating my patients for chronic pain. Suddenly the government took an aggressive stance on the use of opioids and I was charged for over-prescription'. The sudden shift in the federal government's approach meant that he was caught on the wrong side of the law.

2. This factor cut across the professional domain (e.g. accounting and medical standards) and the organizational domain (organizations operating within these standards). For example, one participant explained how the growing pressures to meet professional standards became unwieldy: 'The level of stress and pressure to meet our targets was bad enough, forget about the procedural checks and balances. And it got worse over the years. It was not about right or wrong but what helped us meet our business goals. No one got rewarded for being compliant, but you got punished for not meeting your targets'. This highlights the disconnect between professional standards and organizational targets.

3. Participants explained how they faced tensions between making business and ethical decisions. 'We were spending more and more money and time on compliance and transparency. There was so much pressure and when push came to shove, we made decisions based on cost and benefit analysis—the only thing anyone cared about at the end of the day'. As a result, there was a conflation of cost/benefit decisions with ethical decisions: 'Ethical decisions should be binary—right or wrong, not grey like a business case', one participant explained. Another participant said that in his business, 'We were the industry leaders and set the rules and guidelines', but he knew ways to navigate this: 'Clients came to us for advice. I knew the loopholes and never thought anyone was going to ever question me', which again speaks to how people were trying to manage the unwieldy process of mounting regulation within their own unique organizational contexts.

1. Keeping-up with mounting regulatory expectations

2. Tensions between professional standards and organizational targets

3. Conflation of business and ethical decisions

Diagram 10.3 Environmental Milieu Drivers of Professional
Misconduct

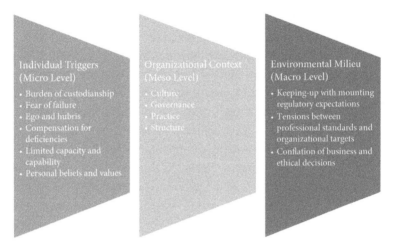

**Individual Triggers
(Micro Level)**

• Burden of custodianship
• Fear of failure
• Ego and hubris
• Compensation for
  deficiencies
• Limited capacity and
  capability
• Personal beliefs and values

**Organizational Context
(Meso Level)**

• Culture
• Governance
• Practice
• Structure

**Environmental Milieu
(Macro Level)**

• Keeping-up with mounting
  regulatory expectations
• Tensions between
  professional standards and
  organizational targets
• Conflation of business and
  ethical decisions

Diagram 10.4 Professional Misconduct: An Outcome of the Layering of
Individual, Organizational, and Environmental Factors

Layering of Individual, Organizational, and Environmental Factors

It is not one simple factor at the individual (e.g. hubris), organizational (e.g. culture), or environmental level (e.g. excessive regulation)
that explains professional misconduct. Instead, it is the dynamic interaction and tension between different levels of analysis that within certain
circumstances mean that all of us can succumb to professional misconduct (see Diagram 10.4). In the same way that addressing climate
change requires changes in behaviour at an individual and household
level (micro), at an organizational and community level (meso), and
at a government and supranational level (macro), so overcoming issues

of misconduct necessitates a collective responsibility to redress norms, incentives, and behaviours at the micro, meso, and macro levels.

The stark reality is that tougher punishments and public vilification of convicted felons do not prevent others from committing misconduct because at the point of wrongdoing individuals are not rationalizing but sleepwalking. Equally, the solution to preventing misconduct is not only a focus on organizational culture or providing the right level of industry regulation that can be meaningfully applied by people with their organizational contexts. The cause and the solution to professional misconduct is to address all three scales of analysis. This is clearly not an easy endeavour, but returning to the ethos of this book there are many reputations at stake, from the large to the minutiae, which require careful management to avoid reputation damage.

The first time I visited the prison where the research was conducted, it was a happy day because it was visiting time; inmates had the opportunity to spend time with their families in the visiting area. Despite the pleasant atmosphere, I found myself looking at a young man sat next to his wife, while their young child crawled around their feet, and wondered how we have come to live in a world where everyday characters like you and me are so close to the pitfalls created by those triggers, contexts, and the wider milieu. This ordinary-looking, family guy, was a reality check for me, that in a flash any of us could slide to the other side of the knife edge and sleepwalk into incarceration, reputation damage, and a life like that of the young man in the prison visiting room. Of course, all of us have experienced some form of reputation damage in our lives, and how we recover from it and rebuild it in our own contexts is a personal journey. There are important lessons from the extreme context of these seventy inmates that give us an insight into how best we can re-establish ourselves.

11

Recovering From Reputation Damage

Reputation damage is something that all of us face at different stages of our lives. This is true of us as individuals as well as for our organizations. It can vary from a minor setback related to our performance to a crisis related to our behaviour (Huegens et al., 2004; Sims, 2009). In the best case scenario, reputation damage is temporary and different groups give us the benefit of the doubt, particularly if the activity was considered not entirely our fault or within the realms of our control. In contrast, significant reputation damage ensues when our actions are considered as ethically or morally wrong and relate to professional misconduct (Greve et al., 2010).

Reputation damage is important to understand because it is something that we all experience in different guises and because it has an impact on others, including family members, friends, acquaintances, and colleagues. It is also something that if we prepare for, we can somewhat, although not entirely, limit the damage (Coombs and Holladay, 2006). The degree of reputation damage will depend on whether others consider the episode is related to one's *capability*, which relates to perceptions of quality and performance, or *character*, which relates to one's incentives and behavioural tendencies (Mishina et al., 2012). Waller and Younger (2017: 16–17) provide a helpful distinction:

> For an individual, your capability reputation derives from how well you are perceived to be fulfilling a specific task. On the other hand, character reputation reflects moral and social qualities, including openness, honesty and transparency. Reputations for capability are inherently sticky, in marked contrast to character reputations, which are more volatile.

Reputations at Stake. William S. Harvey, Oxford University Press. © William S. Harvey (2023).
DOI: 10.1093/oso/9780192886521.003.0011

The fact that the authors describe capability reputations as 'sticky' reveals that stakeholders may be willing to overlook certain ethical behaviours if performance (capability) is strong. However, perceptions related to capability are sticky because once investors, customers, or employees do not believe in the quality of your product, service, or work then this becomes difficult to change—the reputation has changed and is stuck. While capability and character are relevant considerations that stakeholders use based on the past, they do not give us much indication about the future. This is relevant in the context of reputation damage because in rebuilding a reputation there is nothing you can do about the past, but a lot you can do about the future in relation to recovery. I will return to this later in the chapter when I introduce the concept of *contribution*.

When we damage our reputation, it is not only about the mounting negative perceptions that other stakeholders hold about us (based on our past capabilities and character, as well as their bleak assessment of our ability to provide future contributions), it is also about the triggering of identity loss and transition. Identity—how we see ourselves—is considered a progenitor of reputation (Foreman et al., 2012). Identity loss is triggered by events (Ashforth, 2011), trauma (Maitlis, 2009), and changes at work (Pratt et al., 2006) which can lead to individuals feeling disorientated, lacking connection and questioning the meaning of their lives. This period when a reputation has been severely damaged can be described as a liminal transition period where individuals are coming to terms with who they were, who they are, and who they are becoming (Conroy and O'Leary-Kelly, 2014; Brown, 2015).

People who experience severe reputation damage face the challenge of shrugging off their old identities, which were the cause of their demise, and developing their new identities, which can be a source of revival (Dutton et al., 2010). There are three phases of identity transition. First is separation, which is detachment from the old sense of self. Second is transition, which is overcoming a state of ambiguity and indeterminacy. Third is reincorporation, which is developing a new sense of self (Kennett-Hensel et al., 2012). During periods of identity transition, individuals often define 'ideal selves', attributes which they would like to possess, and 'ought selves', attributes which they feel they should possess

(Higgins, 1987). Often people rely on feedback from others to help with their transition, for example a psychologist, mentor, or friend. However, sometimes people are unable to receive feedback because they do not have the financial resources, the relevant networks, or the ability to trust feedback from others. Or, in the case of inmates, to which I now turn, there are obvious structural limits to having sustained conversations with people outside of the prison.

How Inmates Are Planning their Recovery

One of the benefits of extreme contexts is they can help us to build theory and understanding through clearly visualizing a situation (Pettigrew, 1990), including developing models of success and failure (Eisenhardt, 1989b). With this in mind, I return to the context of the seventy inmates of a US Federal Prison, based on research led by my colleague, Navdeep Arora. This group had evidently all dramatically damaged their reputations because they were serving prison sentences and were at different stages of thinking about and planning how to rebuild their identities.

Navdeep and I identified three overlapping phases that explain how inmates experienced the process of recovering from reputation loss (see Diagram 11.1). These phases intersect and are not always linear because sometimes people improve and at other times they regress as they deal with their despondency, loss of identity, and the limitations of imprisonment, and dare to plan for their recovery. We were able to map each of our seventy participants to one of these stages.

Diagram 11.1 Three Overlapping Phases of Recovery

Phase 1: Despondency and Loss of Identity

The initial phase is a devastating, emotional, and traumatic psychological experience for participants. This is inflamed by the severing of ties that people experience from their families, friends, and social network, alongside the often high level of exposure of their incarceration on mass and social media channels. During this initial eighteen- to twenty-four-month period, inmates are still coming to terms with their loss of employment and career prospects alongside the financial burden of legal expenses. Participants described the experience as an emotional rollercoaster where there is a mixture of denial, shame, and shock of what has just happened. Seventeen of the seventy participants were at this stage when we spoke to them. As one person stated, 'Forget about my reputation, I didn't even know who I was at that time'. Another participant described the experience as being 'sucked into a black hole' where 'nothing I said mattered anymore and no one wanted to say anything to me'. Many said in the build-up to their trials, they resorted to drinking heavily. Others found themselves having to seek out psychiatric help. Two-thirds of participants faced family discord including marital strife, separation, divorce, or ostracism. One participant said that his wife divorced him within two weeks of sentencing and while leaving the courthouse his brother said 'he wanted nothing to do with me anymore'.

Phase 2: Acceptance, Self-Realization, and Transition

After hitting the bottom of the dark abyss, we start to witness participants (thirty out of the seventy we interviewed) beginning to heal as they accept responsibility for their past actions and begin to see a way to climb out. This is a precarious transition period, as inmates are simultaneously trying to shrug off their old identities, come to terms with their current identities, and start planning how to forge new identities. One participant captures this constant tension between the past, 'I am still getting over my shock', present, 'worrying about my family, appealing my case in the court, struggling with life as a prisoner', and future, 'and [I'm] worried about how I am going to earn a living in the future with the label of "a felon".

Because participants had a lack of contact with the outside world, they create what is known as construed image, which is an impression of what they think others think of them (Brown et al., 2006), drawing on the limited information they have from outside the prison: 'I have spoken with old clients and colleagues and they have been kind of elusive', 'They are willing to work with me but not sure how their partners and customers will react to my conviction. I can relate to that because I was in their shoes once … So, I try to read between the lines and gauge how they are thinking about me'. The problem with using construed image is when individuals have been through a difficult phase, there can be a tendency to think the worst, particularly when external signals are limited and ambiguous.

The second approach participants took in this phase was to start informal dialogue and sharing of their experiences with fellow inmates. As one participant said, 'I have been able to get some good insights from some of the fellow inmates who were in the same industry for a number of years, are much more experienced and have given me valuable ideas for how I can reshape my future'. Many participants acknowledged one of their advantages was time: 'I am working on a business plan with help from a couple of guys here who used to be successful entrepreneurs themselves'. And they looked for support from their peers: 'They know what to look for in a plan'. They also tended to reciprocate by helping others: 'I am in turn helping some people who want to go back to school for higher education'.

Phase 3: Thinking and Planning Recovery

The third phase involves twenty-three participants developing their thinking around how to recover from their reputation damage. Building on their prior construed image, participants start to develop mental maps for the future. These mental maps fall into three categories: born again, remediate, and disguise. The trajectory of their mental maps for how they plan to climb out of the dark abyss is determined by how they fell. One participant reflects on his fall and climb:

> It was very difficult to even picture the future in the beginning, but when you speak to others like yourself, and read about the booming economy, you get excited about what you can contribute with your experience and capabilities. Once you see the light at the end of the tunnel, you start painting a picture for yourself and working towards it. I know it is going to change as I talk to more people but at least I have a direction.

Beyond thinking about their recovery, we found that participants start to plan, albeit within the confines of their circumstances, through education, retraining, and networking. One participant, for example, was working towards his PhD so he can teach what he has learned over the past thirty years. Another participant is leveraging his doctorate in mathematics combined with his training in medicine to develop new models for investment management.

The Way You Fall Affects How You Climb

It was clear that the way that participants damaged their reputation impacted on how they managed to recover. There were three aspects of how people fell from grace: the process, prominence, and proximity. First, process is determined by the severity and frequency of the events, the time elapsed since the reputation damaging events, and the length of the sentence. One participant explained to Navdeep that his criminal case started three years before his sentencing where he had no income, no access to his assets, and he was treated like a 'third class citizen'. He said that he had two years left of his sentence and it was difficult to be positive about changing people's perceptions when for five years all he has heard are negative sentiments. Hence, the length of time related to the fall influences the climb.

The second factor that impacts recovery from reputation damage is prominence. One participant was candid about how the prominence of his legal case made it difficult to escape:

> We made headlines in several local newspapers and the television for six months. Everyone knew about it, even my friends in other countries.

Another participant explained that there were over 700 employees and hundreds of clients in his company. In the past he had 'regarded [him]self as the chief custodian and overseer of [employee] livelihoods and interests'. He went on to explain that he had benefitted financially and in status which helped him to build a strong reputation in the industry as well as in his local community. However, that visibility—referred to as the burden of celebrity (Wade et al., 2008)—was also a contributor to how hard he fell from grace. One inmate said that because his case was highly visible, his fall was 'big and noticeable. I have a large hole to climb out of'. In some cases, it was not only the reputation damage to the person and their organization, but also to their wider set of stakeholders such as customers and suppliers, which added weight to their fall and also created a greater burden for the climb in the knowledge that so many people were affected. In other cases, a public sector leader and a physician both said that their prior accomplishments, including being in leadership positions, supporting charities, and winning professional and community awards, were used to sensationalize the story of misconduct and thus hardened the fall. In the words of the physician:

> My arrest was staged with full fanfare. Three television stations, and multiple news reporters were ready with their cameras when they escorted me out. I made the headlines on the 6pm daily news. It was all bad—not a mention of what I had achieved in the past.

The third factor that influenced recovery from reputation damage was proximity, which was the level of access and connection participants

had to stakeholders. While they were all obviously limited in their communications with stakeholders while incarcerated, there was significant
variation and we found that those with more limited proximity found
it harder to rebuild. Proximity had three parts to it. First, the obviously limited access to communication with stakeholders meant that
participants were unclear around their perceptions and intentions. As
one participant stated, 'Ex-business colleagues are cautiously concerned
about communicating with me and saying too much, and I can understand that'. Second, there were limits in how far participants could build
up their capability through education or professional experience. One
participant said that he was keen to remain productive within prison,
and he gained a lot of reward from teaching students to help them
obtain their high school diploma. However, he said there was 'nothing to help me keep my capabilities fresh and relevant', which was a
missed opportunity because with the current level of education and
professional experience in the prison, 'we could contribute a lot and
keep ourselves relevant while serving our sentences'. Third, the lack of
potential employment and income weighed heavily on the minds of participants. They mentioned how not having any income while in prison
was painful and they also worried: 'How do you demonstrate your ability to contribute when you have been out of the market for four to five
years?'

In short, process, prominence, and proximity can either improve
or worsen recovery from reputation damage (see Diagram 11.2). As I
mentioned above, all of us hold a construed image of what we believe
others think of us and this is particularly salient when either we do
not have access or choose not to receive feedback from others. Construed image shapes the mental maps of how individuals intend to
climb out of their dark abyss. Consequently, the mental maps that they
create to climb are shaped by their fall. We found that participants
used a variety of belays to help them climb, ranging from institutional (e.g. affiliations), organizational (e.g. networks and deploying
their expertise), and personal (e.g. family and friends). The strength
and extent of this support also lessened the fall when participants
slipped.

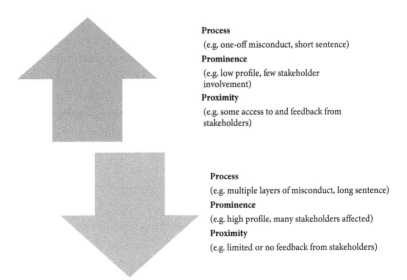

Process
(e.g. one-off misconduct, short sentence)
Prominence
(e.g. low profile, few stakeholder involvement)
Proximity
(e.g. some access to and feedback from stakeholders)

Process
(e.g. multiple layers of misconduct, long sentence)
Prominence
(e.g. high profile, many stakeholders affected)
Proximity
(e.g. limited or no feedback from stakeholders)

Diagram 11.2   How Process, Prominence, and Proximity can Improve or Worsen Recovery From Reputation Loss

Contribution Is the Most Important Anchor to Climb

It is well known that character and capability are important aspects for both reputation damage and repair (Mishina et al., 2012; Waller and Younger, 2017; Park and Rogan, 2019). Almost all of the participants that we researched had been affected by character reputation, and everyone expressed in strong terms that they recognized that it would be a long and painful process to rebuild their character reputations. One person commented that when he arrived at the prison another inmate said he would struggle to rub off the 'F' on his head, which referred to the 'Felon' label that undermines perceptions of a character. As one participant candidly explained:

Once you are a felon, your character is tarnished for life. It is a stigma that some people carry forever. It will remain at the back of people's minds when they are interacting with you. Some of my life-long friends have stopped talking to me, and ex-business colleagues have written me off. I really cannot depend upon convincing people that my character has improved.

Another participant said he hoped that if he showed how he was giving back to his family and the community over time others will forgive and change their opinion of him. One participant said that repairing his reputation started by taking responsibility for his past actions, followed by forgiving himself and being 'pragmatically transparent' and 'owning up' with others.

Capability reputation was an area that participants were focused on improving. Professionals who had previously worked in regulated sectors such as medicine, law, and banking made plans to pivot their capabilities into other areas such as consulting and teaching. Often the thought and the planning around pivoting came from discussions with other inmates. Those who already worked in non-regulated sectors such as consulting and start-ups focused less on changing sector and more on the area within the sector. One participant who previously worked in real estate was clear about the areas where he could and could not work:

I will never be able to raise a real estate fund again, but I am not prohibited from managing real estate such as single family housing and commercial properties, or teaching others how to do it. I did it very successfully for years, and can build a great future around it.

Seven participants said that they planned to invest in their education through MBA, executive and PhD training to help them transition into new areas. Technology skills was a recurring theme that participants recognized they needed to keep updated. They also saw technology as a means to reconstruct their reputation online, and around nineteen participants were writing papers, books, or articles for publication when they were released. Despite the benefits of technology for rebuilding their reputation, participants recognized that it was a double-edged sword because being prominent via mass media and social media platforms had exacerbated their reputation damage. Therefore, they were reflecting pragmatically on how they could focus on the positive aspects of their messaging to help 'neutralize negative press' from the past.

Notwithstanding the significance of capability and character reputation, we found there was an overwhelming emphasis by participants on their contribution, which means projecting how they can provide value to others in the future. The reason for this is that capability and character were considered more a reflection of their past behaviours, whereas contribution was focused on how others perceived they could positively contribute in the future. In the words of one optimistic real estate agent: 'I can start contributing to any company that manages large real estate and deliver results immediately. This will be my ticket to rebuilding my life'. Another participant was clear about the relative merits of contribution compared to character and capability:

> People are not going to wait for me to show them that my character is improving, or if my capabilities from three years ago are still relevant. Character and capability matter when people think about your past, but they are more interested in what you can do to contribute to them in the future.

One participant said that others are willing to forget about your prior negative reputation if they stand to benefit from you. Another participant said that if his contribution can rise to a certain level then his character reputation becomes merely a secondary consideration. Other aspects that inmates considered important in relation to contribution were immediately showing their relevance, delivering results to people, being meaningful to, and making up for the harm they had done to their families.

What Can We Learn From Inmates About Recovering From Reputation Damage

The insights from these seventy inmates reveal the major challenges they faced in terms of damage to their reputations and with their recovery. Although participants were devastated by their situation, they recognized that this presented an opportunity to better themselves. In other words, a reputation damaging event, however difficult the experience is at the time, can be a potential source for reflection and positive renewal. Or, as one participant said, 'I am grateful for this nightmare in my life. I am a much better person now'. Another participant said: 'When I look back, I was making a lot of money, but I was unhappy. I want to rebuild my reputation as a happy person with a successful family and life, not someone with a lot of money. I would still be beating the same drum if this had not happened to me'. A new measure of success, which included happiness, would be the focus of his recovery.

There was an acknowledgment from participants that their nightmare experiences had been an important part of not just their recovery, but their betterment. As one participant aptly summarized: 'I don't want to regain my old identity; I want to build a new one that I am proud of'.

12

Concluding Remarks

Recap

Throughout this book, I have argued that multiple reputations are at stake. I started by focusing on the bigger picture of why we should care about reputation, highlighting both the risks and the rewards, and the relevance from the macro level for countries and governments through to the meso level for organizations and the micro level for individuals. I began by looking at the importance of reputation from the bigger picture for governments, countries, regions, cities, and organizations operating across international borders, before looking at the importance and challenges for organizations of managing reputation. The last three chapters focused on the individual level, from the role of leaders in managing reputation to what we can learn from individuals who have committed misconduct and are seeking to recover.

Why should we care about reputation? As discussed in Chapter 1, reputation can have both rewards for those who engage and costs for those who abscond. There can also be different gradations of rewards and risks, depending on the speed and scope of the event. The virtual events company Hopin, for example, started with four employees in 2020 and was valued at $2 billion in less than a year (Bradshaw and Kruppa, 2020). The downfall for organizations and leaders can also be steep. Theranos, the American health technology corporation, was valued at $10 billion in 2013 and 2014, but when researchers, journalists, and authorities started to question the validity of its technology, the company took a downward spiral and was eventually dissolved. In 2018, the founder and CEO Elizabeth Holmes, as well as the President and Chief Operating Officer Ramesh Balwani, were both charged with fraud by the US Securities and Exchange Commission. Hence, a second reason

Reputations at Stake. William S. Harvey, Oxford University Press. © William S. Harvey (2023).
DOI: 10.1093/oso/9780192886521.003.0012

we should care about reputation is because it has impact at all levels: for governments, organizations, and individuals.

What is stakeholder capitalism and how does it relate to reputation? The rising relevance of stakeholder capitalism, in which organizations orientate themselves to serve the interests of all their stakeholders, has now become an important consideration for governments. Different forms of reputation are important for governments, including the reputation of the party, the leader, or the policies that are being advocated, as discussed in Chapter 2. We know that there are major existential threats that the world faces, from climate change to unprecedented levels of inequality. There is a moral duty for leaders to address these issues with urgency and there are reputational reasons why they should be managed. Intermediaries, such as popular and social media, influence how we perceive organizations and their leaders. If the public sniff they are being duped by rhetoric or vagueness (as was the media's response to Downing Street's denial of a Christmas Party in December 2020 when there was a UK-wide lockdown), then external analysis will be damning.

How does the reputation of place drive the movement of tourists, migrants, and investment? There has been a proliferation of rankings and reviews of places that inform impressions among different groups. Intermediaries again play an important role in influencing people's perceptions of and mobilities to different places. These can range from films, documentaries, and photos of places to the role of government departments, recruitment firms, and migration agents. Such intermediaries not only influence people moving to places for the first time, but also the return of citizens living and working abroad to their home countries.

How does reputation impact organizations operating across international borders? Through supply chains, the sales of their products and services, and through the location of their offices and employees, their geographic reach means that inevitably global organizations face the challenge of having multiple and competing reputations. This requires careful management, particularly in an era of social media and influencers where news can travel swiftly. The scope of reputation is blurring geographic boundaries, meaning that the location of an event can quickly have an impact in other parts of the world. Digital devices are also blurring the boundaries between work and social lives, meaning that the conduct of a leader or an employee outside of office premises or during work hours can impact on the reputation of the organization at breakneck speeds.

How do you manage a reputation across borders with the competing demands of your stakeholders? I have drawn on examples from four sectors (telecommunications, housing, mining, and libraries) in four countries (Zimbabwe, India, Madagascar, and the UK) to explain that navigating the needs of different stakeholders is not just an intellectual exercise of identifying important groups, but has vital implications for the ability of organizations to operate and survive. The management of reputation among different stakeholders is a central part of being considered credible and ethical.

What about purpose? There has been a growing emphasis on the purpose of the organization. Organizations need to align their purpose with relevant external trends such as social movements around equality, diversity, and inclusion. There also needs to be alignment between an organization's purpose and its values, otherwise what leaders espouse will not be reflected in the behaviours of its employees. Although there is a lot of rhetoric around purpose, values, and behaviours, for there to be positive reputational outcomes they need to be meaningful and relevant, particularly for employees as well as for other stakeholders.

How do we deal with threats? Every organization faces reputation threats. This does not mean that they all must deal with a crisis. In fact, the crises that we witness in the public domain tend to be the exception rather than the norm. However, it is important to recognize that every organization and individual faces threats. Typically, these entail some form of disconnect or disruption between their identity (how they perceive themselves) and reputation (how others perceive them). Strong leadership by example and demonstrable cultural change in behaviours across the organization are two ways to credibly redress reputation threats.

Why should we do good and cultivate responsible reputations? Because doing good means doing well. This has been brought to the fore through the challenges the coronavirus pandemic has inflicted on many people's lives, particularly those from disadvantaged backgrounds. I drew on a breadth of examples including Surfwell, the health and wellbeing initiative in Devon and Cornwall Police, community leadership among the Konyaks of Nagaland, and Daoist nothingness among SME leaders in China. These wide-ranging illustrations emphasize the benefits in different geographic and cultural contexts of reflective and responsible forms of leadership, even when on the surface they do not always appear to illustrate doing good.

Why is the risk of reputation damage so high? All of us have the potential to commit professional misconduct and therefore significantly damage our reputation. When we hear stories in the news or read press releases, the impression is often that it is another employee who has gone rogue or a leader who has overstepped the mark. The uncomfortable truth is that our behaviours are a function of individual triggers that stem from our personal circumstances, the organizational context in which we are working within such as culture and behavioural norms, and the wider environmental milieu such as regulation and industry standards. It is the layering of the individual, organizational, and environmental that explains why individuals act unethically and unlawfully, and therefore succumb to reputation damage.

How does one repair and rebuild a damaged reputation? All organizations and individuals face various forms of reputation damage throughout the course of their life. While the research conducted with Navdeep Arora on inmates who had committed professional misconduct is an extreme case study, there are important lessons for us all about how we can recover. The process of acceptance, self-realization, and transition is not a linear or easy path during or after prison. The way that people fall from grace has an impact on their ability to rebuild, which has valuable lessons for why we need to safeguard our reputations, but not at all costs. Finally, while character and capability reputation play an important role in how others make judgements about us, it is worth highlighting that our contribution—how we propose to provide value to others in the future—is an important part of the recovery process.

Reputations at Stake

The thrust of my argument is that reputations are at stake. There are reputation consequences for countries, cities, regions, organizations of all forms (governments, corporations, private firms, and family businesses) and individuals. There is little room for absconding from reputation because absence will mean that you lose any control of the narrative, whether you are representing a political party seeking election, a chief executive leading a publicly listed company, or an employee applying for promotion. Taking little or no pride in one's reputation is equally as problematic as too much. Hubris is undesirable because over-confidence in one's accomplishments and abilities via mass and social media is likely to lead to blind spots and disinterest around the perceptions of others.

Yet a challenging truth to accept is that however hard we might try to present ourselves to the outside world, there is never one single and coherent reputation, but often multiple and competing reputations that require attention and management. In fact, how we want others to think about us, our construed image, will never be entirely the same as how we are perceived: our reputation. This suggests it is even more important to manage and maintain our reputation to avoid it taking on a life of its own. Given the polarization we are witnessing in societies, from elections to vaccines, and climate change to inequality, it means that online echo chambers heighten the risk of civil unrest. Therefore, leaders and organizations must understand and redress the issues that are being raised by different stakeholders.

Reputations are also at stake because of the presence and growing voices of multiple stakeholders. These range from employees to customers, regulators to investors, with every organization needing to consider why, how, and when it engages with them. The relevance of engaging with relevant stakeholders is true of whether we are talking about a phenomenon such as the coronavirus pandemic or a national government such as the US administration representing the disparate needs of groups. Even representatives of regions (such as Silicon Valley) and cities (such as Lima) need to balance global and national issues alongside local concerns, or corporations (such as the State Grid Corporation of China), teams (such as the New Zealand All Blacks), or leaders (such as Ursula von der Leyen, the President of the European Commission) need to put stakeholders at the top of their agendas. I deliberately use these ranging examples at different scales and in various locations to highlight that the notion of *reputations at stake* is neither an esoteric global issue, nor a myopic local one, but one that infuses us all at multiple levels.

Understanding who our different stakeholders are and reflecting on how they are important is an essential mechanism to ensure external and internal alignment. External alignment is recognizing the pressing concerns and ensuring they are captured in our purpose. Internal alignment is ensuring the values and behaviours of our organizations and ourselves are consistent with the purpose that we espouse. I say 'our purpose' loosely because this applies to supranational organizations such as the United Nations, countries such as Myanmar, organizations such as Lego, business leaders such as Jack Ma, and activists such as Greta Thunberg. We may not always like what stakeholders say or do, and at times we may decide to push back, but they are nevertheless a vital source of data that we need to hear, reflect upon, and respond to.

It is clear from the last few years that existential threats such as the climate emergency, biodiversity depletion, unprecedented levels of inequality, and geopolitical and social tensions have been brought into sharp focus through the onset of the coronavirus pandemic. The disparity within and among cities, regions, and countries between the haves and have nots is palpable. We have a moral responsibility for the sake of sustaining the planet and for safeguarding social cohesion to recognize our collective stakes in the world, however small or large. The notion of stakeholder capitalism, which is gaining rapid momentum, is a reflection that a primacy towards one purpose (e.g. financial returns) or one stakeholder (e.g. investors) is both undesirable and creates perverse incentives. For example, for decades many businesses have performed very well for their shareholders, which is one form of economic value for one stakeholder group, but have created destruction for another form of value: natural capital, which is the world's stock of natural resources such as its geology, soils, air, water, and living organisms. All of this has a damaging long-term impact on every stakeholder, including investors.

All of this is to say that reputation envelops everything we do; it operates at multiple levels and therefore is too far-reaching to ignore. The stakeholder capitalism movement and the emphasis on alignment of organizational purpose to external societal trends and to internal values and behaviours is just one manifestation of the importance and value of reputation. Reputation is all around us and hard to escape as children and adults, from how we behave, perform in exams, secure jobs and promotions, and contribute to life in our communities. Our reputations even impact on the mundane such as our ability to book a taxi via Uber, secure holiday accommodation via Airbnb, or in my case the ability to sell this book. In all three cases, the experience of others will lead to a score and sometimes a review, which may influence how others perceive you in relation to future transactions. This is what David Waller and Rupert Younger (2017) aptly refer to in the title of their book *The Reputation Game: The Art of Changing How People See You.*

What Can We Do? Some Cautionary Recommendations

Building on the evidence and examples in this book, I conclude by providing some cautionary recommendations (see Diagram 12.1). Cautionary because they are not easy to accept or implement and they require temperament.

1. Because reputation pervades every aspect of government, business, and society, it requires our attention and management. However, it should not be over-engineered because excessive self-promotion can have the opposite outcome to its intent. In particular, there is the risk that too much self-promotion is perceived as self-serving, which erodes trust among different groups.

2. Draw on sources of information outside of our immediate comfort zone. Our go-to sources of information (e.g. radio and television shows, newspapers, magazines, newsfeeds, etc.) are the trusted spaces where we go for information, analysis, and commentary. However, by relying on the same sources we are less likely to challenge our thinking and behaviour because they reinforce many of the things we already believe and have been doing. Widening where we seek information and analysis, but always questioning the veracity of our source, helps to enhance our thinking, foster innovation, and implement compelling policies

that are relevant for broader groups. This is likely to become even more salient as artificial intelligence, gamification, and the metaverse blur the boundaries between humans and machines, and the real world and virtual worlds.

3. Obtain feedback from (and understand the perceptions of) different stakeholders. It is tempting to rely only on our inner network of family members, friends, and colleagues, but we know from the social networks literature that while they are trusted sources, they limit our understanding of the world around us. This can potentially blinker our policies and behaviours. Widening the reach of who we speak to and receive feedback from can help us to become more aware of how our actions may influence both reputation opportunities and risks.

4. Acknowledge that migration brings reputation benefits at all levels. This includes for governments and organizations who require skills and labour supply, for businesses and society who benefit from different training, perspectives, cultures, and norms. As we have seen with governments across the world, from Singapore to the US and the UAE to the UK, the reputation benefits of attracting and retaining foreign talent are significant; however there can be political and social backlash in relation to integration, accommodation, jobs, infrastructure, and services. Hence, policies and narratives require careful reputation management by leaders of governments, organizations, and communities.

5. Accept that the challenge of having multiple and competing reputations should not be confused with pleasing everyone at the same time. This is an unrealistic utopia. That said, it is important to acknowledge that a much wider set of groups have a stake in the organization. These stakeholders are affected by the policies, products, services, and behaviours of organizations and can influence how they are perceived. A proactive engagement with the various and differing stakeholders over time helps leaders and organizations to understand and behave according to their wider responsibilities to people and the planet.

6. Leaders and organizations should demonstrate tangible initiatives that demonstrate their commitment to responsibility. In

the context of green initiatives that relate to the environment or blue initiatives that relate to social issues, leaders of governments, corporations, and other organizations have communicated their commitment via speeches and reports, but tangible and/or substantive actions have been much slower to follow. It is clear that the public are growing tired of empty promises, statements, and what Greta Thunberg famously referred to as 'blah blah blah'. Cocreate reputation with others and work with them to endorse the claims you make through your thought leadership activity. This involves engaging with your employees and other trusted stakeholders to identify what the organization should be known for. This ensures alignment between what you think and what others think about the reputation of your organization. It also helps with your marketing, public relations, and social media activity because these trusted groups can help to endorse your claims in the public domain.

7. Developing your reputation does not necessarily need to be done alone. In fact, other people play an important role in showcasing your reputation through the conversations they have with others, through the references they write, and through the public statements they make. All of these help to endorse any claims you make around your reputation, which are more credible when they are corroborated by others.

8. Balance the aspiration to build and sustain reputations with multiple stakeholders, while (perhaps paradoxically) avoiding the mentality of focusing and preserving reputation at all costs. While the benefits and the costs of reputation are too great to ignore and therefore require leaders and organizations to prioritize, it is essential that we avoid the trap of overly focusing on reputation so that it becomes about impression management and communications rather than identifying, reflecting, and delivering on a meaningful purpose.

9. Build resilience within organizations through avoiding unduly relying on prominent leaders. We know that leaders can be both an asset and a burden to organizations, particularly if they are founders and celebrity leaders who receive significant attention

from customers, the media, and investors. Widening the influence of other members of the organization helps to strengthen governance structures, widens levels of responsibility, avoids too much power being wielded by a small number of people, and helps to mitigate risk if a problem arises with a leader.

10. Draw on the external environment as a strong guide around the relevance of an organization's purpose. This is true for governments writing their manifestos and white papers as it is for organizations developing their strategies. Events that occur in the external environment such as social movements (e.g. Black Lives Matter, #MeToo, Occupy, etc.) provide a mirror to ask leaders whether their purpose as an organization is aligned with the expectations of people across society. While an obsession with the external environment can be an unnecessary distraction, it can provide insights around the relevance of the organization.

11. Take positive steps to support employees, wider sets of stakeholders, and the environment. I am not referring to tokenistic gestures, however appreciated, that focus on short-term impression management benefits, rather meaningful and sustained impact. Of course, meaningful and sustained impact can be financially and operationally costly, and seen as a distraction. However, meaningful steps to support employees and wider groups can lead to unexpected financial and reputation benefits as well as acts of reciprocity.

12. My final recommendation is to channel the negative aspect of reputation setbacks and damage into a positive source of renewal. Inevitably, the process and outcome of reputation loss is a time of frustration, sadness, and regret. The impact can lead to financial loss, the folding of a business, and the destruction of one's identity. Witnessing the experiences of the inmates made me realize that despite the major reputation setbacks for these individuals, reputation loss can also trigger a turning point for learning, hope, betterment, happiness, and fulfilment.

Recommendation 1: Proactive reputation management without over-engineering.

Recommendation 2: Engaging with broader sources of information, while uncomfortable, can bring enhanced thinking, innovation and policy.

Recommendation 3: Feedback from different stakeholders makes us aware of both opportunities and risks related to our reputations.

Recommendation 4: Migration brings reputation benefits at all levels, and requires balancing with challenges related to integration, accommodation, jobs, infrastructure and services.

Recommendation 5: Multiple and competing reputations is not about pleasing everyone at the same time, but addressing that different groups rightly have a stake in the organisation.

Recommendation 6: Showing tangible initiatives to demonstrate commitment to responsibility and providing less vacuous statements such as greenwashing and bluewashing which engender widespread scepticism.

Recommendation 7: Co-create reputation with others and work with them to endorse the claims you make through your thought leadership activity.

Recommendation 8: Balance the aspiration for building and sustaining a positive reputation with multiple stakeholders, but avoid the mindset of preserving your reputation at all costs.

Recommendation 9: Founders and leaders can bring major reputation benefits for organizations, but are also a major source of vulnerability which calls for widening the influence of others.

Recommendation 10: External social movements and internal behaviours can be seen as a distraction, but provide early clues of areas that require change in the organization's purpose.

Recommendation 11: Positive actions for employees, stakeholders and the environment can be costly and appear out of scope in the short-term, but can reap financial and reputation rewards in the long-term.

Recommendation 12: Reputation damage is a time of frustration, sadness and regret, but can mark a turning point for learning, hope, betterment, happiness and fulfilment.

Diagram 12.1 Cautionary Recommendations

I hope that the above recommendations provide a moment to reflect and a source of inspiration for recognizing the multiple reputations at stake for us all. Whether we like it or not, reputation (while not something to unduly obsess over) does require us all to take collective responsibility, whether we are government or business leaders, managers, employees, volunteers, members of communities, or many of these. We must attend to reputation proactively and meaningfully. If managed effectively, our reputation can have positive and sustained outcomes for wider sets of stakeholders, future generations, and our planet.

References

Abbott, A. (2021) 'COVID's Mental-health Toll: How Scientists Are Tracking a Surge in Depression', *Nature*, 590, pp. 194–195.

Abidin, C. (2015) 'Communicative Intimacies: Influencers and Perceived Interconnectedness', *Ada: A Journal of Gender, New Media, & Technology*, 8. Available at: http://adanewmedia.org/2015/11/issue8-abidin/.

Ashforth, B.E. (2011). *Role Transitions in Organizational Life: An Identity-Based Perspective*. Mahwah, NJ: Lawrence Erlbaum Associates.

Avolio, B.J. and Gardner, W.L. (2005) 'Authentic Leadership Development: Getting to the Root of Positive Forms of Leadership', *The Leadership Quarterly*, 16(3), pp. 315–338.

B Corporation (2021) *About B Corps*. Available at: https://bcorporation.net/about-b-corps.

Barnett, M. L., Jermier, J. M., and Lafferty, B. A. (2006) 'Corporate Reputation: The Definitional Landscape', *Corporate Reputation Review*, 9(1), pp. 26–38.

Barnett, M. L. and A. J. Hoffman. (2008) 'Beyond Corporate Reputation: Managing Reputational Interdependence', *Corporate Reputation Review*, 11(1), pp. 1–9.

Barney, J. B. (1986) 'Organizational Culture: Can It Be a Source of Sustained Competitive Advantage?' *Academy of Management Review*, 11(3), pp. 656–665.

Basdeo, F.K., Smith, K.G., Frimm, C.M., Rindova, V.P., and Derfus, P.L. (2006) 'The Impact of Market Actions on Firm Reputation', *Strategic Management Journal*, 27(12), pp. 1205–1209.

Beaverstock, J. V. (2002) 'Transnational Elites in Global Cities: British Expatriates in Singapore's Financial District', *Geoforum*, 33(4), pp. 525–538.

Bebchuk, L.A., Kastiel, K., and Tallarita, R. (2022) 'Stakeholder Capitalism in the Time of COVID', *SSRN*. Available at: http://dx.doi.org/10.2139/ssrn.4026803.

Bitektine, A. (2011) 'Toward a Theory of Social Judgments of Organizations: The Case of Legitimacy, Reputation, and Status', *Academy of Management Review*, 36(1), pp. 151–179.

Bogdanich, W. and Forsythe, M. (2018) 'How McKinsey Lost Its Way in South Africa', *The New York Times*, 26 June. Available at: https://www.nytimes.com/2018/06/26/world/africa/mckinsey-south-africa-eskom.html.

Bourne, H. and Jenkins, M. (2013) 'Organizational Values: A Dynamic Perspective', *Organization Studies*, 34(4), pp. 495–514.

Boutyline, A. and Willer, R. (2017) 'The Social Structure of Political Echo Chambers: Variation in Ideological Homophily in Online Networks', *Political Psychology*, 38(3), pp. 551–569.

Bower, J. L. and Paine, L. S. (2017) 'The Error at the Heart of Corporate Leadership', *Harvard Business Review*, 95(3), pp. 50–60.

Bradshaw, T. and Kruppa, M. (2020) 'Virtual Events Developer Hopin's Valuation Jumps to $2bn', *Financial Times*. 10/11/2020. Available at: https://www.ft.com/content/c79bc717-0c5b-43eb-8595-0073169a1728.

British Academy. (2018) *Reforming Business for the 21st Century. A Framework for the Future of the Corporation*. Available at: https://www.thebritishacademy.ac.uk/documents/76/Reforming-Business-for-21st-Century-British-Academy.pdf.

Brown, T.J., P.A. Dacin, M.G. Pratt, and D.A. Whetten. (2006) 'Identity, Intended Image, Construed Image, and Reputation: An Interdisciplinary Framework and Suggested Terminology', *Journal of the Academy of Marketing Science*, 34(2), pp. 99–106.

Brown, A., and Scribner, T. (2014) 'Unfulfilled Promises, Future Possibilities: The Refugee Resettlement System in the United States', *Journal on Migration and Human Security*, 2(2), pp. 101–120.

Brown, A. D. (2015) 'Identities and Identity Work in Organizations', *International Journal of Management Reviews*, 17(1), pp. 20–40.

Burns, J.M. (1978) *Leadership*. Perennial, New York.

Business Roundtable. (2019) 'Our Commitment'. Available at: https://opportunity.businessroundtable.org/ourcommitment/.

Bustos, E. O. (2021). Organizational Reputation in the Public Administration: A Systematic Literature Review. *Public Administration Review*, 81(4), pp. 731–751.

Chambers, E. G., Foulon, M., Handfield-Jones, H., Hankin, S. M., and Michaels, E. G. (1998) 'The War for Talent', *McKinsey Quarterly*, 3, pp. 44–57.

Chan, W. (1970) *A Source Book in Chinese Philosophy*. Princeton, NJ: Princeton University Press.

Charity Commission. (2022) 'Press Release. Official Report Criticises Former Trustees of Kids Company'. Available at: https://www.gov.uk/government/news/official-report-criticises-former-trustees-of-kids-company.

Chatman, J. (1991) 'Matching People and Organizations: Selection and Socialization in Public Accounting Firms', *Administration Science Quarterly*, 36(3), pp. 459–484.

Chen, X. P. and Chen, C. C. (2004) 'On the Intricacies of the Chinese Guanxi: A Process Model of Guanxi Development', *Asia Pacific Journal of Management*, 21, pp. 305–324.

Chen, T., Li, F. and Leung, K. (2017) 'Whipping Into Shape: Construct Definition, Measurement, and Validation of Directive-achieving Leadership in Chinese culture', *Asia Pacific Journal of Management*, 343, pp. 537–563.

Chyxx. (2019) 'Review of the Development of China's Logistics Industry in 2018 and Analysis of Industry Development Trends in 2019'. Available at: http://www.chyxx.com/industry/201910/798460.html.

Citarella, J. (2021) 'Are We Ready for Social Media Influencers Shaping Politics?', *The Guardian*, 24 April. Available at: https://www.theguardian.com/commentisfree/2021/apr/24/social-media-influencers-shaping-politics.

Clifford, S. (2009) 'Video Prank at Domino's Taints Brand', *The New York Times*, 16 April. Available at: https://www.nytimes.com/2009/04/16/business/media/16dominos.html.

Condon, C. and Torres, C. (2021) 'Fed Ethics Questions Spread to Barkin on McKinsey's Opioid Role', *Bloomberg*, 30 September. Available at: https://www.bloomberg.com/news/articles/2021-09-30/fed-ethics-questions-spread-to-barkin-on-mckinsey-s-opioid-role.

Conroy, S.A., and O'Leary-Kelly, A.M. (2014) 'Letting Go and Moving On: Work-Related Identity Loss and Recovery', *Academy of Management Review*, 39(1), pp. 67–87.

Coombs, W.T. and Holladay, S.J. (2006) 'Unpacking the Halo Effect: Reputation and Crisis Management', *Journal of Communication Management*, 10(2), pp. 123–127.

Covaleski, M., Dirsmith, M., Heian, J., and Samuel, S. (1998) 'The Calculated and the Avowed. Techniques of Discipline and Struggles Over Identity in Big Six Public Accounting Firms', *Administrative Science Quarterly*, 43(2), pp. 293–327.

Dawkins, J. (2004) 'Corporate Responsibility: The Communication Challenge', *Journal of Communication Management*, 9(2), pp. 108–119.

Deephouse, D. L. (2000) 'Media Reputation as a Strategic Resource: An Integration of Mass Communication and Resource-based Theories', *Journal of Management*, 26(6), pp. 1091–1112.

Dempsey, H., Beioley, K. and Palma, S. (2022) 'Glencore to Plead Guilty to Bribery Charges and Pay $1.5bn Penalty', *Financial Times*, 24/5/2022. Available at: https://www.ft.com/content/1dcb279f-8cd1-4538-9e28-d5a0b74195e5.

Donaldson, T., and Preston, L. E. (1995) 'The Stakeholder Theory of the Corporation: Concepts, Evidence, and Implications', *Academy of Management Review*, 20(1), pp. 65–91.

Dowling, G. R. (2016) 'Defining and Measuring Corporate Reputations', *European Management Review*, 13(3), pp. 207–223.

Dutt, C. and Ninov, I. (2016) 'Tourists' Experiences of Mindfulness in Dubai, United Arab Emirates (UAE)', *Journal of Travel & Tourism Marketing*, 33(8), pp. 1195–1212.

Dutton, J. E., Roberts, L. M., and Bednar, J. (2010) 'Pathways for Positive Identity Construction at Work: Four Types of Positive Identity and the Building of Social Resources', *Academy of Management Review*, 35(2), pp. 265–293.

(The) Economic Times. (1992) 'An Upright Builder Needs Honest Clients to be Successful', 20 December.

(The) Economist. (2019) 'What Companies Are For. Competition, Not Corporatism, Is the Answer to Capitalism's Problems', 22 August. Available at: https://www.economist.com/leaders/2019/08/22/what-companies-are-for

(The) Economist. (2021a) 'Facebook is Nearing a Reputational Point of No Return', 9 October. Available at: https://www.economist.com/leaders/2021/10/09/facebook-is-nearing-a-reputational-point-of-no-return.

(The) Economist. (2021b) 'They Think It's All Over. Europe's Super League Scores a Spectacular Own Goal', 22 April. Available at: https://www.economist.com/business/2021/04/22/europes-super-league-scores-a-spectacular-own-goal.

(The) Economist. (2021c) 'Tracking Space Debris is a Growing Business', 18 September. Available at: https://www.economist.com/science-and-technology/tracking-space-debris-is-a-growing-business/21804756.

(The) Economist. (2022) 'Why Is It So Easy to Hide Dirty Money in Britain? The Rise and Fall of Londongrad', 12 May. Available at: https://www.economist.com/films/2022/05/12/why-is-it-so-easy-to-hide-dirty-money-in-britain.

Earl, S. and Waddington, S. (2013) *Brand Vandals: Reputation Wreckers and How to Build Better Defences.* London: Bloomsbury.

Edgecliffe-Johnson, A., Hill, A., and Kuchler, H. (2021) 'The Big Read. McKinsey. "It Needs to Change its Culture": Is McKinsey Losing its Mystique?', *Financial Times*, 23/02/2021. Available at: https://www.ft.com/content/63f24181-aee0-49f4-9966-a447d79692f0

Eisenhardt, K. M. (1989a) 'Agency Theory: An Assessment and Review', *Academy of Management Review*, 14(1), pp. 57–74.

Eisenhardt, K. M. (1989b) 'Building Theories From Case Study Research', *Academy of Management Review*, 14(4), pp. 532–550.

Elkington, J. (1997) *Cannibals with Forks: The Triple Bottom Line of 21st Century Business.* Oxford: Capstone.

Ellen MacArthur Foundation. (2021) 'Concept. What is a Circular Economy? A Framework for an Economy That Is Restorative and Regenerative by Design'. Available at: https://www.ellenmacarthurfoundation.org/circular-economy/concept.

Enacting Purpose Initiative. (2020) 'Enacting Purpose Within the Modern Corporation: A Framework for Boards of Directors'. Available at: https://www.enactingpurpose.org/assets/enacting-purpose-initiative—eu-report-august-2020.pdf.

Enacting Purpose Initiative. (2021) 'Directors and Investors: Building on Common Ground to Advance Sustainable Capitalism'. Available at: https://www.enactingpurpose.org/assets/epi-report-final.pdf.

Enke, N. and Borchers, N. S. (2019) 'Social Media Influencers in Strategic Communication: A Conceptual Framework for Strategic Social Media Influencer Communication', *International Journal of Strategic Communication*, 13(4), pp. 261–277.

Enrich, D. and Abrams, R. (2020) 'McDonald's Sues Former C.E.O., Accusing Him of Lying and Fraud', *The New York Times*, 10 August. Available at: https://www.nytimes.com/2020/08/10/business/mcdonalds-ceo-steve-easterbrook.html.

Etter, M., Ravasi, D., and Colleoni, E. (2019) 'Social Media and the Formation of Organizational Reputation', *Academy of Management Review*, 44(1), pp. 28–52.

Facebook. (2021) 'Our Mission'. Available at: https://about.facebook.com/company-info/.

Farh, J.L. and Cheng, B.S. (2000) 'A Cultural Analysis of Paternalistic Leadership in Chinese Organization', in J.T. Li, A.S. Tsui, and E. Weldon, (eds) *Management and Organizations in the Chinese Context.* London: Macmillan, pp. 94–127.

Featherstone, J. (2022) 'Don't Lose Your Head', in M. Witzel, (ed.) *Leadership in Crisis.* Abingdon: Routledge.

Featherstone, J. and Harvey, W.S. (2021) 'Tough and Kind Leadership Among the Konyaks of Nagaland', *Journal of Global Responsibility*, 12(1), pp. 52–61.

Federal Bureau of Investigation. (2016) 'International Corruption. U.S. Seeks to Recover $1 Billion in Largest Kleptocracy Case to Date', 20 July. Available at: https://www.fbi.gov/news/stories/us-seeks-to-recover-1-billion-in-largest-kleptocracy-case-to-date.

Fitri, A. (2022) 'How President Zelensky's Approval Ratings Have Surged', *The New Statesman*, 1 March. Available at: https://www.newstatesman.com/chart-of-the-day/2022/03/how-president-zelenskys-approval-ratings-have-surged.

Florida, R. (2005) *Cities and the Creative Class*. New York: Routledge.

Fombrun, C.J. (1996) *Reputation. Realizing Value from the Corporate Image*. Boston, Massachusetts: Harvard Business School Press.

Fombrun, C.J. (2012) 'The Building Blocks of Corporate Reputation: Definitions, Antecedents, Consequences', in M.L. Barnett and T.G. Pollock, (eds) *The Oxford Handbook of Corporate Reputation*. Oxford: Oxford University Press, pp. 94–113.

Foreman, P.O., Whetten, D.A., and Mackey, A. (2012) 'An Identity-based View of Reputation, Image, and Legitimacy: Clarifications and Distinctions Among Related Constructs', in M.L. Barnett and T.G. Pollock, (eds) *The Oxford Handbook of Corporate Reputation*. Oxford: Oxford University Press, pp. 179–200.

Fortune. (2021) '100 Best Companies to Work For'. Available at: https://fortune.com/best-companies/2021/.

Free, C. and Macintosh, N. (2008) 'A Research Note on Control Practice and Culture at Enron', M.J. Epstein and J.Y. Lee, (eds) *Advances in Management Accounting (Advances in Management Accounting*, Vol. 17). Bingley: Emerald Group Publishing Limited, pp. 347–382.

Freberg, K., Graham, K., McGaughey, K., and Freberg, L. A. (2011) 'Who Are the Social Media Influencers? A Study of Public Perceptions of Personality', *Public Relations Review*, 37(1), pp. 90–92.

Freeman, R. E., Harrison, J. S., Wicks, A. C., Parmar, B. L., and De Colle, S. (2010) *Stakeholder Theory: The State of the Art*. Cambridge: Cambridge University Press.

Gabbioneta, C., Faulconbridge, J.R., Currie, G., Dinovitzer, R., and Muzio, D. (2019) 'Inserting Professionals and Professional Organizations in Studies of Wrongdoing: The Nature, Antecedents and Consequences of Professional Misconduct', *Human Relations*, 72(11), pp. 1707–1725.

Moore, D. (2001) 'Bush Job Approval Highest in Gallup History. Widespread Public Support for War on Terrorism', *Gallup*, 24 September. Available at: https://news.gallup.com/poll/4924/bush-job-approval-highest-gallup-history.aspx

Garrison-Jenn, N. (2005) *Headhunters and How to Use Them*. London: The Economist and Profile Books.

Gast, A., Illanes, P., Probst, N., Schaninger, B., and Simpson, B. (2020) 'Purpose: Shifting From Why to How', *McKinsey Quarterly*, 22 April. Available at: https://www.mckinsey.com/business-functions/organization/our-insights/purpose-shifting-from-why-to-how.

Gladwell, M. (2002) 'The Talent Myth. Are Smart People Overrated?' *The New Yorker*, July 22. Available at: https://www.newyorker.com/magazine/2002/07/22/the-talent-myth.

Glassdoor. (2022) 'Best Places to Work 2022'. Available at: https://www. glassdoor.co.uk/employers/awards/best-places-to-work/?_gl=1*or83lw*_ga* MTM1MDI0MjI4MS4xNjUzMDQ4NTAw*_ga_RC95PMVB3H* MTY1MzA1Mjk2OS4yLjAuMTY1MzA1Mjk2OS42MA.

Glückler, J. and Armbrüster, T. (2003) 'Bridging Uncertainty in Management Sonsulting: The Mechanisms of Trust and Networked Reputation', *Organization Studies*, 24(2), pp. 269–297.

Goffee, R. and Jones, G. (2000) 'Why Should Anyone Be Led By You?', *Harvard Business Review*, 78(5), pp. 62–70.

Gopinath, C.Y. (2019). 'The Builder Who Refused to Bribe', Medium. Available at: https://medium.com/@humbird/the-builder-who-refused-to-bribe-6f88a34788ca

Gotsi, M., and Wilson, A. M. (2001) 'Corporate rRputation: Seeking a Definition', *Corporate Communications: An International Journal*, 6(1), pp. 24–30.

Graffin, S. D., Bundy, J., Porac, J. F., Wade, J. B., and Quinn, D. P. (2013) 'Falls From Grace and the Hazards of High Status: The 2009 British MP Expense Scandal and its Impact on Parliamentary Elites', *Administrative Science Quarterly*, 58(3), pp. 313–345.

Granovetter, M. S. (1973) 'The Strength of Weak Ties', *The American Journal of Sociology*, 78(6), pp. 1360–1380.

Grant, A. (2013) *Give and Take. A Revolutionary Approach to Success*. New York: Viking, Penguin Group.

Gray, E. R. and Balmer, J. M. (1998) 'Managing Corporate Image and Corporate Reputation', *Long Range Planning*, 31(5), pp. 695–702.

Greve, H.R., Palmer, D., and Pozner, J. (2010) 'Organizations Gone Wild: The Causes, Processes, and Consequences of Organizational Misconduct', *Academy of Management Annals*, 4(1), pp. 53–107

Groutsis, van den Broek, D. and Harvey, W.S. (2015) 'Transformations in Network Governance: The Case of Migration Intermediaries', *Journal of Ethnic and Migration Studies*, 41(10), pp. 1558–1576.

Guess, A. M., Barberá, P., Munzert, S. and Yang, J. (2021) 'The Consequences of Online Partisan Media', *Proceedings of the National Academy of Sciences*, 118(14), pp. 1–8.

Guthridge, M., Komm, A., and Lawson, E. (2008) 'Making Talent a Strategic Priority', *McKinsey Quarterly*, 1, 49–59.

Hampel, C. E., Tracey, P., and Weber, K. (2020) 'The Art of the Pivot: How New Ventures Manage Identification Relationships With Stakeholders as They Change Direction', *Academy of Management Journal*, 63(2), pp. 440–471.

Harvey, W.S. (2011a) 'British and Indian Scientists Moving to the U.S', *Work and Occupations*, 38(1), pp. 68–100.

Harvey, W.S. (2011b) 'How Do University of Oxford Students Form Reputations of Companies?', *Regional Insights*, 2, pp. 12–13.

Harvey, W.S. (2012). Brain circulation to the UK? Knowledge and investment flows from highly skilled British expatriates in Vancouver. *Journal of Management Development*, 31(2): 173–186.

Harvey, W.S. and Morris, T. (2012) 'A Labor of Love? Understanding Reputation Formation Within the Labour Market', in M.L. Barnett and T.G. Pollock, (eds) *The Oxford Handbook of Corporate Reputation*. Oxford" Oxford University Press, pp. 341–360.

Harvey, W.S., Parry, S. and Vorbach, P. (2014) 'Managing Leadership and Cultural Change at Beak and Johnston: A Work in Progress', *Global Business and Organizational Excellence*, 33(6), pp. 43–50.

Harvey, W.S. and Groutsis, D. (2015) 'Reputation and Talent Mobility in the Asia Pacific', *Asia Pacific Journal of Human Resource Management*, 53(1), pp. 22–40.

Harvey, W.S. and Mitchell, V.W. (2015) 'Marketing and Reputation Management in Professional Service Firms', in L. Empson, D. Muzio, J. Broschak, and B. Hinings, (eds) *The Oxford Handbook of Professional Service Firms*. Oxford: Oxford University Press, pp. 279–303.

Harvey, W.S., Morris, T., and Müller Santos, M. (2017a) 'Reputation and Identity Conflict in Management Consulting', *Human Relations*, 70(1), pp. 92–118.

Harvey, W.S., Tourky, M., Knight, E., and Kitchen, P. (2017b) 'Lens or Prism? How Organisations Sustain Multiple and Competing Reputations', *European Journal of Marketing*, 51(4), pp. 821–844.

Harvey, W.S., Groutsis, D., and van den Broek, D. (2018) 'Intermediaries and Destination Country Reputation: Explaining Flows of Skilled Migration', *Journal of Ethnic and Migration Studies*, 44(4), pp. 644–662.

Harvey, W.S., Beaverstock, J.V., and Li, H. (2019) 'Common Threats and Managing Reputation in Executive Search Firms', *British Journal of Management*, 30(4), pp. 847–868.

Harvey, W.S. and Witzel, M. (2020) 'How We Formed a Strategy—and then Adapted it to a Global Pandemic', *Board Agenda*. Available at: https://boardagenda.com/2020/07/08/how-we-formed-a-strategy-and-then-adapted-it-to-a-global-pandemic/.

Harvey, W.S., Morris, T., and Smets, M. (2020) 'Reputation Management in Professional Service Firms', in Christoph H. Vaagt, (ed.) *Law Firm Strategies for the 21st Century*. 2nd Edition. London: Globe Law and Business, pp. 199–216.

Harvey W.S. and Arora, N.K. (2021) 'Educating Incarcerated Professionals: Challenges and Lessons From an Extreme PhD Context', *Journal of Management Inquiry*, 30(4), pp. 461–467.

Harvey, W.S. (2021a) 'Managing Multiple and Conflicting Reputations in Global Organizations', AIB Insights, 21(3). Available at: https://insights.aib.world/article/24454-managing-multiple-and-conflicting-reputations-in-global-organizations.

Harvey, W.S. (2021b) 'Why and How Leaders Can Navigate Reputation Among Multiple Stakeholders', in M. Witzel, (ed.) *Leadership in Crisis*. Abingdon: Routledge, pp. 147–155.

Harvey, W.S., Osman, S., and Tourky, M. (2021c) 'Building Internal Reputation From Organisational Values', *Corporate Reputation Review*, 25, pp.19–32.

Harvey, W.S., Mitchell, V-W., Almeida Jones, A., and Knight, E. (2021d) 'The Tensions of Defining and Developing Thought Leadership Within Knowledge-intensive Firms', *Journal of Knowledge Management*, 25(11), pp. 1–33.

Hayward, M. L., Rindova, V. P., and Pollock, T. G. (2004) 'Believing One's Own Press: The Causes and Consequences of CEO Celebrity', *Strategic Management Journal*, 25(7), pp. 637–653.

Hawkings, B., Bailey, A., Coles, T., Harvey, W.S., Smart, A., and Waters, H. (2019) 'Unlimited Value. Leading Practice in Unlimited Value Creation', *Arts Council England*. Available at: https://www.artscouncil.org.uk/sites/default/files/download-file/Unlimited-Value-Report.pdf.

Higgins, E. T. (1987) 'Self-discrepancy: A Theory Relating Self and Affect', *Psychological Review*, 94(3), pp. 319–340.

Hill, C. W. and Jones, T. M. (1992) 'Stakeholder-agency Theory', *Journal of Management Studies*, 29(2), pp. 131–154.

Hoejmose, S. U., Roehrich, J. K., and Grosvold, J. (2014) 'Is Doing More Doing Better? The Relationship Between Responsible Supply Chain Management and Corporate Reputation', *Industrial Marketing Management*, 43(1), pp. 77–90.

Hofstede Insights. (2021) 'What About Malaysia?' Available at: https://www.hofstede-insights.com/country/malaysia/.

Hopkinson, P. and Harvey, W.S. (2019) 'Lessons From Ellen MacArthur and the Circular Economy on How Leaders can Build and Sustain Transformation?' *The European Business Review*, March–April 2019, pp. 65–69.

Heugens, P.P., Van Riel, C.B., and Van Den Bosch, F.A. (2004) 'Reputation Management Capabilities as Decision Rules', *Journal of Management Studies*, 41(8), pp. 1349–1377.

Independent Inquiry Child Sexual Abuse. (2021) 'Child Protection in Religious Organisations and Settings'. Available at: https://www.iicsa.org.uk/publications.

IoD. (2019) 'IoD Manifesto. Corporate Governance'. Available at: https://www.iod.com/Portals/0/PDFs/Campaigns%20and%20Reports/Corporate%20Governance/IoD%20Manifesto%20-%20Corporate%20Governance.pdf?ver=2019-11-19-082215-783.

Jenkins, P. (2022) 'The New ESG Realpolitik and the Fossil Fuel Bonanza', *Financial Times*, 16 May. Available at: https://www.ft.com/content/217b6462-f977-4075-a236-ef96fac91505?emailId=62831cfeb1a4c7002361cbed&segmentId=22011ee7-896a-8c4c-22a0-7603348b7f22.

Jensen, M. and Meckling, W. (1976) 'Theory of the Firm: Managerial Behavior, Agency Costs, and Ownership Structure', *Journal of Financial Economics*, 11, pp. 5–50.

Kegan, R. and Lahey, L. L. (2009) *Immunity to Change. How to Overcome It and Unlock Potential in Yourself and Your Organization*. Boston, MA: Harvard Business Press.

Kennett-Hensel, P. A., Sneath, J. Z., and Lacey, R. (2012) 'Liminality and Consumption in the Aftermath of a Natural Disaster', *Journal of Consumer Marketing*, 29(1), pp. 52–63.

Kings College London. (2020) 'Assessing the Mental Health and Wellbeing of the Emergency Responder Community in the UK'. Available at: https://kcmhr.org/erreport2020-mentalhealth-wellbeing/

Klar, D. (2019) 'Corporate Knights. The Voice for Clean Capitalism. 50+ Real World Examples of Private Sector SDG Leadership', *Corporate Knights*. Available at: https://www.corporateknights.com/?sponsors_post=50-real-world-examples-private-sector-sdg-leadership.

Kolhatkar, S. (2018) 'McKinsey's Work for Saudi Arabia Highlights its History of Unsavory Entanglements', The New Yorker, 1 November. Available at: https://www.newyorker.com/news/news-desk/mckinseys-work-for-saudi-arabia-highlights-its-history-of-unsavory-entanglements#:~:text=McKinsey's%20Work%20for%20Saudi%20Arabia%20Highlights%20its%20History%20of%20Unsavory%20Entanglements,-By%20Sheelah%20Kolhatkar&text=For%20most%20of%20McKinsey%20%26%20Company's,and%20professionalism%20in%20its%20work .

Krows Digital. (2020) 'Marketing Case Study #2: Daniel Wellington Social Media Strategy'. Available at: https://krows-digital.com/influencer-marketing-daniel-wellington-marketing-case-study-2/ .

Lange, D., Lee, P. M., and Dai, Y. (2011) 'Organizational Reputation: A Review', *Journal of Management*, 37(1), pp. 153–184.

Lange, D., Bundy, J. N., and Park, E. (2020) 'The Social Nature of Stakeholder Utility', *Academy of Management Review*, 47(1).

Laufer, W. S. (2003). Social accountability and corporate greenwashing. *Journal of Business Ethics*, 43(3), 253–261.

Lenton, T. M., Rockström, J., Gaffney, O., Rahmstorf, S., Richardson, K., Steffen, W., and Schellnhuber, H. J. (2019) 'Climate Tipping Points—Too Risky to Bet Against', *Nature*, 575, pp. 592–595.

Libraries Unlimited. (2021) 'Annual Report 2020/2021. Bringing Ideas, Imagination, Information and Knowledge to People's Lives and Communities'.

Lin, N. (2001) *Social Capital. A Theory of Social Structure and Action*. Cambridge: Cambridge University Press.

Li, H., Harvey, W.S., Jones, O., and Yang, J. (2021) 'A Daoist Perspective on Leadership: Reputation-building in Chinese SMEs', *International Journal of Entrepreneurial Behavior & Research*, 27(1), pp. 279–300.

Livesey, C. (2011) 'Defining the Mass Media', *Sociology Central*. Available at: http://www.sociology.org.uk/notes/media_defined.pdf.

Lim, J. S. and Young, C. (2021) 'Effects of Issue Ownership, Perceived Fit, and Authenticity in Corporate Social Advocacy on Corporate Reputation', *Public Relations Review*, 47(4), pp. 102071.

Lovelace, J. B., Bundy, J., Hambrick, D. C., and Pollock, T. G. (2018). 'The Shackles of CEO Celebrity: Sociocognitive and Behavioral Role Constraints on "Star" Leaders', *Academy of Management Review*, 43(3), pp. 419–444.

Lovelace, J. B., Bundy, J. N., Pollock, T., and Hambrick, D. (2021) 'The Push and Pull of Attaining CEO Celebrity: A Media Routines Perspective', *Academy of Management Journal*, 65(4).

Maak, T., Pless, N.M., and Voegtlin, C. (2016) 'Business Statesman or Shareholder Advocate? CEO Responsible Leadership Styles and the Micro-foundations of Political CSR', *Journal of Management Studies*, 53(3), pp. 463–493.

MacDonald, J. S. and MacDonald, L. D. (1964) 'Chain Migration Ethnic Neighborhood Formation and Social Networks', *The Milbank Memorial Fund Quarterly*, 42(1), pp. 82–97.

Maclean, M., Harvey, C., and Kling, G. (2017) 'Elite Business Networks and the Field of Power: A Matter of Class?' *Theory, Culture & Society*, 34(5–6), pp. 127–151.

Maddocks, S. (2020) 'A Deepfake Porn Plot Intended to Silence Me: Exploring Continuities Between Pornographic and "Political" Deep Fakes', *Porn Studies*, 7(4), pp. 415–423.

Maitlis, S. (2009) 'Who Am I Now? Sense Making and Identity in Post-traumatic Growth', in L.M. Roberts and J.E. Dutton, (eds) *Exploring Positive Identities and Organizations: Building a Theoretical and Research Foundation*. New York: Routledge, pp. 47–76.

Malnight, T. W., Buche, I., and Dhanaraj, C. (2019) 'Put Purpose at the Core of Your Strategy', *Harvard Business Review*, 97(5), pp. 70–78.

March, J. G. and Simon, H. A. (1958) *Organizations*. New York: Wiley.

Mayer, C. (2020) 'It's Time to Redefine the Purpose of Business. Here's a Roadmap', *World Economic Forum*. Available at: https://www.weforum.org/agenda/2020/01/its-time-for-a-radical-rethink-of-corporate-purpose/.

McPherson, M., Smith-Lovin, L., and Cook, J.M. (2001) 'Birds of a Feather: Homophily in Social Networks', *Annual Review of Sociology*, 27(1), pp. 415–444.

McVea, J. F. and Freeman, R. E. (2005) 'A Names-and-faces Approach to Stakeholder Management How Focusing on Stakeholders as Individuals Can Bring Ethics and Entrepreneurial Strategy Together', *Journal of Management Inquiry*, 14, pp. 57–69.

Michaels, E., Handfield-Jones, H., and Axelrod, B. (2001) *The War for Talent*. Harvard Business Press.

Mishina, Y., Block, E. S., and Mannor, M. J. (2012) 'The Path Dependence of Organizational Reputation: How Social Judgment Influences Assessments of Capability and Character', *Strategic Management Journal*, 33(5), pp. 459–477.

Mitchell, R. K., Agle, B. R., and Wood, D. J. (1997) 'Toward a Theory of Stakeholder Identification and Salience: Defining the Principle of Who and What Really Counts', *Academy of Management Review*, 22(4), pp. 853–886.

Moir, L. (2001) 'What Do We Mean by Corporate Social Responsibility?' *Corporate Governance*, 1(2), pp. 16–22.

NASA. (2021) 'Space Debris and Human Spacecraft'. Available at: https://www.nasa.gov/mission_pages/station/news/orbital_debris.html.

Norman, W. and MacDonald, C. (2004) 'Getting to the Bottom of "Triple Bottom Line"', *Business Ethics Quarterly*, 14(12), pp. 243–262.

Muzio, D., Faulconbridge, J., Gabbionetta, C., and Greenwood, R. (2016) 'Bad Apples, Bad Barrels and Bad Cellars. A "Boundaries" Perspective on Professional Misconduct', in D. Palmer, K. Smith-Crowe, and R. Greenwood, (eds) *Organizational Wrongdoing*. Cambridge: Cambridge University Press, pp. 141–175.

Olegario, R., Harvey, W.S., and Mueller, M. (2011a) 'QMM/Rio Tinto in Madagascar. Case A: Protecting the Island's Biodiversity', Oxford University Centre for Corporate Reputation.

Olegario, R., Harvey, W.S., and Mueller, M. (2011b) 'QMM/Rio Tinto in Madagascar. Case B: Engaging with Local Communities', Oxford University Centre for Corporate Reputation.

Park, B. and Rogan, M. (2019) 'Capability Reputation, Character Reputation, and Exchange Partners' Reactions to Adverse Events', *Academy of Management Journal*, 62(2), pp. 553–578.

Paul, K. (2021) 'Facebook Announces Name Change to Meta in Rebranding Effort', The Guardian, 28 October. Available at: https://www.theguardian.com/technology/2021/oct/28/facebook-name-change-rebrand-meta

Pettigrew, A. M. (1990) 'Longitudinal Field Research on Change: Theory and Practice', *Organization Science*, 1(3), pp. 267–292.

Piketty, T. (2014) *Capital in the Twenty-first Century*. Cambridge, MA: The Belknap Press of Harvard University Press.

Police Firearms Officers Association. (2017) 'Police Mental Health Sickness up by 47%'. Available at: https://www.pfoa.co.uk/blog/police-mental-health-sickness-up-by-47.

Pollock, T. G., Lashley, K., Rindova, V. P., and Han, J. H. (2019) 'Which of These Things Are Not Like the Others? Comparing the Rational, Emotional, and Moral Aspects of Reputation, Status, Celebrity, and Stigma', *Academy of Management Annals*, 13(2), pp. 444–478.

Polman, P. and Winston, A. (2021) *Net Positive. How Courageous Companies Thrive by Giving More Than They Take*. Boston, MA: Harvard Business Review Press.

Porter, M. E. (2000) 'Location, Competition, and Economic Development: Local Clusters in a Global Economy', *Economic Development Quarterly*, 14(1), pp. 15–34.

Porter, M.E. and Kramer, M.R. (2006) 'Strategy and Society: The Link Between Competitive Advantage and Corporate Social Responsibility', *Harvard Business Review*, 84 (12), pp. 78–92.

Pratt, M. G., Rockmann, K.W., and Kaufmann, J.B. (2006) 'Constructing Professional Identity: The Role of Work and Identity Learning Cycles in the Customization of Identity Among Medical Residents', *Academy of Management Journal*, 49(2), pp. 235–262.

Pruzan, P. (2001) 'Corporate Reputation: Image and Identity', *Corporate Reputation Review*, 4(1), pp. 50–64.

PwC. (2018) 'From Promise to Reality: Does Business Really Care About the SDGs? And What Needs to Happen to Turn Words Into Action?' Available at: https://www.pwc.com/gx/en/sustainability/SDG/sdg-reporting-2018.pdf.

Ravasi, D., Rindova, V., Etter, M., and Cornelissen, J. (2018) 'The Formation of Organizational Reputation', *Academy of Management Annals*, 12(2), pp. 574–599.

RepTrak® 100. (2021) 'Global RepTrak® 100'. Available at: https://www.reptrak.com/rankings/

Rhee, M. and Kim, T. (2012) 'After the Collapse: A Behavioral Theory of Reputation Repair', in M. L. Barnett and T. G. Pollock, (eds) *The Oxford Handbook of Corporate Reputation*. Oxford: Oxford University Press, pp. 446–465.

Rindova, V. P., Williamson, I. O., Petkova, A. P., and Sever, J. M. (2005) 'Being Good or Being Known: An Empirical Examination of the Dimensions, Antecedents, and Consequences of Organizational Reputation', *Academy of Management Journal*, 48(6), pp. 1033–1049.

Rindova, V. P., Williamson, I. O., and Petkova, A. P. (2010) 'Reputation as an Intangible Asset: Reflections on Theory and Methods in Two Empirical Studies of Business School Reputations', *Journal of Management*, 36(3), pp. 610–619.

Roberts, P. W. and Dowling, G. R. (2002) 'Corporate Reputation and Sustained Superior Financial Performance', *Strategic Management Journal*, 23(12), pp. 1077–1093.

Ross, S. A. (1973) 'The Economic Theory of Agency: The Principal's Problem', *American Economic Review*, 63(2), pp. 134–139.

Roulet, T. J. and Clemente, M. (2018) 'Let's Open the Media's Black Box: The Media as a Set of Heterogeneous Actors and Not Only as a Homogenous Ensemble', *Academy of Management Review*, 43(2), pp. 327–329.

Roulet, T. J. (2020) *The Power of Being Divisive. Understanding Negative Social Evaluations*. Stanford, California: Stanford Business Books, Stanford University Press.

Rust, R.T., Rand, W., Huang, M-H., Stephen, A.T., Brooks, G., and Chabuk, T. (2021) 'Real-Time Brand Reputation Tracking Using Social Media', *Journal of Marketing*, 85(4), pp. 21–43.

Salt, J. and Stein, J. (1997) 'Migration as a Business: The Case of Trafficking', *International Migration*, 35(4), pp. 467–494.

Saxenian, A. (2002) 'Brain Circulation: How High-Skill Immigrations Makes Everyone Better Off', *The Brooking Review*, 20(1), pp. 28–31.

Saxenian, A. (2007) *The New Argonauts: Regional Advantage in a Global Economy*. Cambridge, MA: Harvard University Press.

Schoenmaker, D. and Schramade, W. (2019) *Principles of Sustainable Finance*. Oxford: Oxford University Press.

Schultz, M., Mouritsen, J. and Gabrielsen, G. (2001) 'Sticky Reputation: Analyzing a Ranking System', *Corporate Reputation Review*, 4(1), pp. 24–41.

Schwab, K. and Vanham, P. (2021a) 'What is Stakeholder Capitalism?', *World Economic Forum*, 22 January. Available at: https://www.weforum.org/agenda/2021/01/klaus-schwab-on-what-is-stakeholder-capitalism-history-relevance/?utm_source=sfmc&utm_medium=email&utm_campaign=2740992_Agenda_weekly-29January2021&utm_term=&emailType=Newsletter

Schwab, K. and Vanham, P. (2021b) *Stakeholder Capitalism. A Global Economy that Works for Progress, People and Planet*. Hoboken, New Jersey: John Wiley & Sons, Inc.

Seele P. (2007) 'Is Blue is the New Green? Colors of the Earth in Corporate PR and Advertisement to Communicate Ethical Commitment and Responsibility. CRR Working Paper 3/2007'.

Seele, P. and Gatti, L. (2017) 'Greenwashing Revisited: In Search of a Typology and Accusation-based Definition Incorporating Legitimacy Strategies', *Business Strategy and the Environment*, 26(2), pp. 239–252.

Sims, R. (2009) 'Toward a Better Understanding of Organizational Efforts to Rebuild Reputation Following an Ethical Scandal', *Journal of Business Ethics*, 90(4), pp. 453–472.

Smith, N. C. (2003) 'Corporate Social Responsibility: Whether or How?', *California Management Review*, 45(4), pp. 52–76.

Statista. (2021) 'Number of Social Network Users Worldwide from 2017 to 2025', *Statista*. Available at: https://www.statista.com/statistics/278414/number-of-worldwide-social-network-users/.

Stayer, R. (1990) 'How I Learned to Let My Workers Lead', *Harvard Business Review*, 68(6), pp. 66–83.

Sutherland, J. (2020) 'Ensuring General Wisdom: The Critical Role Non-executive Directors and Trustees Play in Executive Performance', Lawbook Consulting Ltd T/A LBC Wise Counsel.

Tourky, M., Harvey, W.S., and Badger, L. (2021) 'Quick Wins to Long-term Outcomes. An Evaluation of Surfwell for Promoting the Health and Wellbeing of Police Officers', ESRC IAA. ISBN 978-0902746-50-3.

United Kingdom (UK) Parliament. (2021) 'Taxpayers Set to Lose Tens of £billions in Government's Covid-19 Support Schemes'. Available at: https://committees.parliament.uk/committee/127/public-accounts-committee/news/156186/taxpayers-set-to-lose-tens-of-billions-in-governments-covid19-support-schemes/

United Nations. (2021) 'Department of Economic and Social Affairs: Sustainable Development'. Available at: https://sdgs.un.org/goals.

United States Department of Justice. (2020) 'Justice News. Goldman Sachs Charged in Foreign Bribery Case and Agrees to Pay Over $2.9 Billion'. Available at: https://www.justice.gov/opa/pr/goldman-sachs-charged-foreign-bribery-case-and-agrees-pay-over-29-billion.

Van den Broek, D., Harvey, W.S., and Groutsis, D. (2016) 'Commercial Migration Intermediaries and the Segmentation of Skilled Migrant Employment', *Work, Employment and Society*, 30(3), pp. 523–534.

Velamuri, R., Venkataraman, S., and Harvey, W.S. (2017a) 'Seizing the Ethical High Ground: Ethical Reputation Building in Corrupt Environments', *Journal of Management Studies*, 54(5), pp. 647–675.

Velamuri, R., Harvey, W.S., and Venkataraman, S. (2017b) 'Being an Ethical Business in a Corrupt Environment', *Harvard Business Review*.

Vogel, D. J. (2005) 'Is There a Market for Virtue? The Business Case for Corporate Social Responsibility', *California Management Review*, 47(4), pp. 19–45.

Wade, J. B., Porac, J. F., Pollock, T. G., and Graffin, S. D. (2008) 'Star CEOs: Benefit or Burden?', *Organizational Dynamics*, 37(2), pp. 203–210.

Walker, K. (2010) 'A Systematic Review of the Corporate Reputation Literature: Definition, Measurement, and Theory', *Corporate Reputation Review*, 12(4), pp. 357–387.

Waller, D. and Younger, R. (2017) *The Reputation Game: The Art of Changing How People See You*. London: One World Publications.

Wartick, S. L. (2002) 'Measuring Corporate Reputation: Definition and Data', *Business & Society*, 41(4), pp. 371–392.

Wenning, M. (2011) 'Kant and Daoism on Nothingness', *Journal of Chinese Philosophy*, 38(4), pp. 556–568.

Yale School of Management. (2022) 'Over 300 Companies Have Withdrawn from Russia—But Some Remain'. Available at: https://som.yale.edu/story/2022/over-300-companies-have-withdrawn-russia-some-remain.

Zavyalova, A., Pfarrer, M. D., and Reger, R. K. (2017) 'Celebrity and Infamy? The Consequences of Media Narratives About Organizational Identity', *Academy of Management Review*, 42(3), pp. 461–480.

Index

Tables and diagrams are indicated by an italic *t* and *d* following the page number.

agency theory 26
agenda-setting theory 15, 16*t*

Black Lives Matter 11, 73, 78, 147
bluewashing 50, 148*d*
    meaning of 49
brain circulation 43, 44*d*
brain drain 43, 44, 44*d*
brain gain 43, 44*d*

capability reputations 14, 15, 126, 127,
    134, 135, 136, 141
celebrity leaders 23–4, 108
Certified B Corporations 9, 77*d*, 78–9
character reputations 14, 15, 104*d*, 126,
    127, 134–5, 136, 141
circular economy 10, 77*d*, 78
    core principles 80
    gaining momentum among
    businesses 80
competing stakeholders, navigating
    needs of 58–72
    Libraries Unlimited, lessons from *see*
    Libraries Unlimited
    navigating corruption *see* corruption
    Rio Tinto in Madagascar, lessons
    from 62–4
    summary of navigating competing
    stakeholders 71–2
coronavirus *see* COVID-19
corporate social responsibility (CSR) 9
    cosmetic responses to 49
    evidencing 81
    impression management 49, 81
    meaning of 49
    stakeholder capitalism 9

triple bottom line 78
    UN emphasis on 81
    see also environmental, social and
    governance issues (ESG)
corruption 58–62
    corruption as part of modern
    world 58–9
    framing ethical commitments 61–2
    leveraging mass and social media to
    strengthen ethical messages 62
    mobilizing disaffected stakeholders
    behind ethical behaviour 59–62,
    60*d*
    organizations resisting corruption,
    examples of 59
    stakeholder positions on ethical
    behaviour 60–1, 60*d*
country level reputations 8
COVID-19 12, 67, 68–9, 101, 143
    corporate acquisitions during 49
    existential threat to government 29,
    30, 143
    human response to 112
crises, cross-border 53–7
    employees compromising an
    organization's reputation 54–5
    global geopolitical clashes,
    organizations caught in 56–7
    leaders compromising an orga-
    nization's reputation 53–4,
    55
    reputation damage cutting across
    political and business lines 55–6
customers
    damage to reputation 130, 132
    delivering value to 75*d*, 76

customers (*Continued*)
 greenwashing 103
 negative reputational
  disengagement 2*d*, 4
 social value to 65, 69
damage to reputations *see* reputation
 damage

Daoism, SME leaders in China 107–11
 employees 107–8
 importance of non-action 107, 110
 indirect attention generation 108–9
 leader's behaviour leading to positive
  unintended consequences 109–10
 leader's conduct, reputation 111
 low profile approach 108
 reducing uncertainty by doing
  good 109
 reputation of businesses evolving
  locally 107–8

ego 116*d*, 118, 124*d*
employees
 attitude towards employer's
  reputation 1–2, 41
 behaviour outside the workplace 54
 burden of custodianship 117
 compromising an organization's
  reputation 54–5
 employers, relationship with 27
 former employees, impact of 41
 growing employee expectations 41
 health and wellbeing, importance
  of 96
 see also health and wellbeing
 individuals' reputations within
  organizations 5
 job candidates 5
 negative reputations demotivating
  employees 4
 organizational values 81–4
 people, performance and culture 92
 positive reputations, attract-
  ing/retaining high
  quality 34

positive reputations important for
 morale and productivity 41
rankings where employees nominate
 their organization 77–8
regional level reputations 7–8
reputation benefits from looking after
 employees 96
talent *see* talent
team level reputations 6
environment 10–11, 80, 124, 142
 BP Deepwater Horizon oil spill 4, 7,
  30, 53
 ESG 80
 existential threats 143
 Extinction Rebellion 10, 73
 internet 11
 space debris 10–11
 stakeholder capitalism 10
 UN COP 10, 73, 79
environmental, social and governance
  issues (ESG) 73, 77*d*, 78
 nature of 80–1
 measurement of 81
 responsible supply chain
  management 46
ethical behaviour *see* corruption
expansion as reward for reputation
  3, 34

global financial crisis, managing 100–4
 distinguishing poor behaviour of
  competitors 103
 functional strategies 102–3
 highlighting symbolic capital 102
 impression management approach,
  use of 102
 managing reputation in response to
  common threats 104*d*
 moving upstream and
  downstream 102, 103
 networking 103
 particular threats for executive search
  sector 101
 survival dependent on fundamentally
  different approach 101

global scale of reputation 46–57
  cross-border crises 53–7
  multiple reputations across
    borders 47–9, 48*d*, 139–40, 142
  responsible supply chain
    management 46
  social influencers, reputations 51–3
  social media reputations, dark side
    of 49–51
government
  electing *see* government, electing
  existential threats to 29–31
  past actions, impact of 33
  reputation, importance of 33–4
governments, electing 20–5
  elite networks and connections
    22, 23
  homogenous networks 20–1
  influences on voters 24–5
  leaders and organizations,
    perceptions of 23–4
  partisanship 21–2
  perceptions guiding choice of
    vote 20–1
  reputation impacting voter
    behaviour 34
  social media, influence of 21–2, 24,
    25
  social media influencers 31
  strong and weak ties 20
greenwashing 49, 50, 104, 148*d*
  meaning of 49, 79

health and wellbeing 11, 96–111, 140–1
  Daoist nothingness *see* Daoism, SME
    leaders in China
  Devon and Cornwall Police surfing
    see Surfwell: health and wellbeing
  health and wellbeing as essential for
    organizations 96
  managing global financial crisis *see*
    global financial crisis, managing
  tough and kind forms of leader-
    ship *see* Konyaks of Nagaland,
    leadership and

hubris 23, 116*d*, 118, 124, 124*d*,
    142
identity
  construed image 130, 133, 142
  identity conflict and reputation in
    management consulting 88–90
  identity loss 127, 128, 129
  identity-reputation gaps 88–90, 89*t*,
    90*d*, 95
  identity theory 15, 16*t*
  identity transition 127–8
  organizational identity 82, 84
  progenitor of reputation 127
  reducing gap between identity claims
    and reputation 90*d*

impression management 50, 102,
    146, 147
  CSR 49, 81
  self-serving 62
imprisonment for professional miscon-
    duct *see* professional misconduct;
    reputation damage,
    recovering from
individual reputation 5–6
  founders and leaders 5
  individuals within society 6
  migration decisions, role in 38,
    39–40
  rapidity of reputation downturns 19
institutional theory 15, 16*t*
intermediaries 31–5
  causes, realities, and outcomes of
    reputation 33–4, 33*d*
  importance of reputation 33–4
  mass media 31–2
  see also media/mass media
  nature of 31
  scale of reach of 31
internet
  environment, and 11
  migrants sharing information
    through 37–8
  online actions, impact of 6, 16
  social media *see* social media

investment 27
  attracting investment as reward for
    reputation 2d, 3
  cryptocurrencies 12, 112, 115
  difficulties attracting investment
    2d, 4
  migration 43, 44
  negative reputations creating
    difficulties for attracting 4
  regional level reputations 7–8
  reputation of place 8, 43, 44, 139
  shareholders 27

Konyaks of Nagaland, leadership
    and 104–7
  balancing toughness and
    kindness 106–7, 106d
  leaders' purposeful listening 106
  strong sense of responsibility within
    community 105–6
  tough leadership regime emphasizing
    kindness 105, 106
  toughness, importance of 105

labour market reputation 40–2
  attracting and retaining talent 41
  definition of 40
  former employees, impact of 41
  importance of 41, 42
  reputation of place, affecting 40
  services firms 42
  'war for talent' 40–1
Libraries Unlimited 64–71
  balancing economic and social
    value 65–6
  COVID-19, impact of 67, 68–9
  mission and six core purposes
    67d, 69
  nature of 64–5
  new core objectives 69–71, 70d
  stakeholders 66d
  strategy, revising 67–71
  terminology when formulating
    strategy 68, 68t

meaning of reputation 14–19
  capability and character as key
    aspects 15
  collective evaluation of an entity 14
  definition of reputation 14, 17t
  fragility of reputation 16–17
  multiple and conflicting reputa-
    tions 16–17, 18–19, 33–4, 47–9,
    142
  reputation changing over time 34
  reputation inextricably linked to its
    stakeholders 17–18
  theoretical perspectives, reputation
    defined from 15, 16t
media/mass media 55, 64, 111, 135,
    142
  comparisons of information and
    media stories 32d
  corporate purpose gaining wider
    media traction 76
  heterogeneous and polarizing
    impressions, creating 32, 32d
  influencing perceptions 21–2, 24, 25,
    31–2, 34
  intermediaries, as 31–2, 33
  leaders, attention on 111
  leveraging mass media to strengthen
    ethical messages 62
  multiple institutions and individuals
    creating content 32, 32d
  negative reputations bringing
    unwanted attention 4
  new mass media 21, 24
  social media see social media
  synthesized media/deep fakes 112
metaverse 6, 12, 74, 112, 145
#MeToo 11, 73, 78, 147
migration 36–45, 139
  benefits of 44–5
  destination reputations 38
  forcibly displaced migrants 36
  impact of migrants 34–5
  intermediaries connecting skilled
    migrants with countries 38, 39–40
  labour market reputation 40–2

multiple reputations informing migration choices 39d
reputation as negative role in migration behaviour 43–4
reputation of places 36, 37–9
return migration and brain circulation 42–5

Occupy Wall Street 11, 73, 147
organizations
bluewashing see bluewashing
celebrity leaders 23–4, 108
circular economy, and see circular economy
competing stakeholders see competing stakeholders, navigating needs of
corruption, and see corruption
crisis management see crises, cross-border
CSR see corporate social responsibility (CSR)
employees see employees
environment, and see environment
ESG, and see environmental, social and governance issues (ESG)
existential threats 29–31
global scale of reputation see global scale of reputation
greenwashing see greenwashing
health and wellbeing see health and wellbeing
impression management see impression management
investment see investment
location, importance of 8
maintaining positive reputations see competing stakeholders, navigating needs of
managers and stakeholders 27–9
multiple reputations across borders 47–9, 48d, 139–40, 142
past actions, impact of 33

professional misconduct, growing threat of see professional misconduct
public recognition 3
purpose and values see purpose and values
reputation damage see reputation damage, recovering from
reputation, importance of 6–7, 33–4, 42
reputation, need to manage 7, 18, 41
services organizations, significance of reputation for 42
shareholder primacy, movement away from 9, 26, 74
social media, and see social media
stakeholder capitalism see stakeholder capitalism
stakeholder theory, and see stakeholder theory
suppliers see suppliers
team level reputations 6
threats, and see threats, responding to
values see purpose and values

performance
capability, character, and 126, 127
employees 93–4
financial performance 30, 48
negative reputations leading to poor performance 4–5
organizational values 81
past capability 17t
people, performance and culture 92
phenomena level reputation 9–10
COVID-19 12
social movements 11
technology 12
power and reputation 20–35
electing governments 20–5
existential threats 29–31
intermediaries 31–5
stakeholder capitalism and stakeholder theory 25–99
pricing, positive reputations 3, 34

professional misconduct 112–25, 126, 141
  background on prison project 113–115
  burden of custodianship 117
  causes of professional misconduct 113, 115–17
  compensation for deficiencies 118–19
  culture of the organization 120
  ego and hubris 118
  environmental milieu 122–4, 124d
  evidence of growing professional misconduct 112
  factors in professional misconduct 113
  fear of failure 117–18
  governance of the organization 120–1
  individual triggers of professional misconduct 116d, 117–20
  layering of individual, organizational, and environmental factors 124–5, 124d
  limited capacity and capability 118
  mounting regulatory expectations 122–3
  organizational context 120–1, 122d
  personal beliefs and values 119–20
  practices of the organization 121
  pressures to meet professional standards 123
  preventing 124–5
  professional misconduct, nature of 115
  risk of sliding into 125
  structure of the organization 121
  struggles to keep up with changes 122–3
  technological shifts and work patterns, impact of 112–13
  tensions between business and ethical decisions 123
public recognition, reward of reputation 3

purpose and values 7, 9, 19, 73–85, 140, 143
  business action on purpose 76–81, 77d, 77–81
  corporate purpose 74–6, 75d
  Enacting Purpose Initiative 76–7
  internalizing values through leaders, managers, and employees 83d
  meaning of purpose 26, 68t, 73
  misalignment of society, purpose and values 74d
  multiple groups, corporate purposes furthering 75–6
  organizational values, internalizing 81–5
  organizational values, nature of 81
  profit as one outcome of corporate purpose 76
  purpose and values alignment, resistance to threat 84, 85
  purpose as life blood of organizations 72
  purpose not aligning with values as reputational risk 74
  purpose, values, and identities, alignment of 82d, 143
  societal-purpose gaps leading to external criticism 73

quality of product and services 1, 2d, 48, 93, 94, 127
  capability reputations 15, 126
  negative reputations leading to assumptions of poor quality 4
  repeat custom 34

recommendations, cautionary 144–8, 148d
regional level reputations 7–8
reputation
  aligning purpose and values *see* purpose and values
  attributes of 14
  capability reputations 14, 15, 126, 127, 134, 135, 136, 141

causes, realities, and outcomes
    of 33–4, 33d
character reputations 14, 15, 104d,
    126, 127, 134–5, 136, 141
corruption, and see corruption
crisis management see crises,
    cross-border
damage to see reputation damage,
    recovering from
difficulty of shifting/'stickiness' 19,
    21, 33
effects of 1–2
global scale of see global scale of
    reputation
health 11
importance of 33–4, 138–9
levels of 5–13, 13d
maintaining positive reputations
    see competing stakeholders,
    navigating needs of
meaning of see meaning of reputation
measuring 50
misleading claims, consequences
    of 51
need for careful oversight of 7
organizations, and see organizations
perspectives of 16t
power, and see power and reputation
professional misconduct, grow-
    ing threat of see professional
    misconduct
reputations at stake 141–4
rewards of see rewards of reputation
risks of see risks of reputation
stakeholders, and see stakeholder
    capitalism; stakeholder theory
theorizing reputation 15, 16t
threats to see threats, responding to
valuable intangible currency, as 2d
reputation damage, recovering
    from 126–37, 141
acceptance, self-realization, and
    transition 129–30
capability, episode related to 126–7
character, episode related to 126–7

construed image 130, 133, 142
contribution, importance of 127,
    134–6
degree of reputation damage 126
despondency and loss of identity 129
factors involved in reputation
    damage, significance of 131–3,
    134d
identity loss 127, 128, 129
identity transition 127–8
inmates' planning of
    recovery 128–31
limiting 126
phases of recovery 128–31, 128d
potential source for reflection and
    positive renewal 137
process of reputation damage 131,
    134d
prominence of reputation
    damage 132, 134d
proximity to stakeholders, influence
    of 132–3, 134d
significance of 126
suppliers and customers 132
thinking and planning
    recovery 130–1
reputation of places
    investment 8, 43, 44, 139
    migration see migration
    tourism 7, 36, 139
resource-based theory 15, 16
return migration 42–3, 44
    see also migration
rewards of reputation 2d, 7
    main ways of accruing 3
Rio Tinto in Madagascar 62–4
risks of reputation 2d, 7, 16, 19
    major risks from negative
    reputations 4–5

signalling and impression
    theory 15, 16t
social capital 23
social construction theory 15, 16t
social media 5, 55, 111, 135, 142

social media (*Continued*)
  algorithms determining content to
    view 21–2
  celebrity leaders and
    organizations 24, 108
  coverage of cities and countries 8
  impacting reputation through social
    advocacy 7
  influence of 21–2, 24, 25, 32, 34,
    49–50
  influencers *see* social media
    influencers
  intermediaries, as 31–2, 33
  leaders, attention on 111
  leveraging social media to strengthen
    ethical messages 62
  measuring reputation 50
  migrants sharing information
    through 37–8
  misleading claims, consequences
    of 50–1
  new mass media, as 21
  opportunistic advocacy 7
  organizations' products/services,
    and 18
  overseeing individual behaviour 115
  proliferation of 22
  social media reputations, dark side
    of 49–51
  unwanted attention 4
social media influencers 31
  authentic partnering, importance
    of 52–3
  benefits of using 52
  nature of 51–2
  population reach 51
  reputations, and 51–3
social movements 11, 78, 140, 147,
    148*d*
social networks 21, 22
  elite networks and connections
    22, 23
  homogenous networks 20–1
  labour market reputation, discussion
    of 41

migrants sharing informa-
    tion through internet/social
    media 37–8
social network theories of
    migration 37
strong and weak ties 20
stakeholder capitalism 9–10, 25–6, 48,
    72, 73, 139
  addressing expectations of wider set
    of stakeholders 34–5, 48–9, 58
  environment, and 10
  see also environment
  gaining legitimacy among different
    group 9–10
  gaining traction in business
    community 73
  nature of 9, 25
  people and planet, centrality of 25–6
stakeholder theory 15, 16*t*, 26–9, 48
  inside-out approach to
    stakeholders 27, 28*t*
  managing expectations of
    shareholders 48–9
  outside-in approach to
    stakeholders 27–9, 28*t*
  shift towards 26–7
  triple bottom line, and 78
  wide set of stakeholders 27
stakeholders' competing needs *see* com-
    peting stakeholders, navigating
    needs of
suppliers
  acting unethically 110
  ethical treatment of 75*d*
  organizations managing reputations
    through 46, 47
  reputation damage to 132
  responsible supply chain
    management 46
  supporting 107
Surfwell: health and wellbeing 97–100
  benefits at individual and
    organizational levels 98–100
  challenges remaining 100
  nature of 97–8

positive response of senior leaders
and middle managers 100
promoting workplace mental
health 97
Sustainable Development Goals
(SDGs) 9–10, 77d, 78, 79
businesses supporting 79
nature of 79
sustainable finance 10, 77d

talent
attracting/retaining talent as reward
for reputation 3, 34, 41
important source of competitive
advantage 41
labour market reputation 40–2
over-emphasizing talent 41
regional level reputations, attracting
talent 8
return migration, countries
encouraging 44
'war for talent' 40–1
technology 12, 112
third parties, endorsement by 62, 90
threats, responding to 86–95, 140
endorsement of third parties 90
identity-reputation gaps 88–90, 89t,
90d, 95

individual level threats, examples
of 86–7
leadership and cultural change in
meat processing 91–5
managing reputation in response to
common threats 104d
organizational level threats, example
of 87
professional misconduct, growing threat of see professional
misconduct
purpose and values alignment,
resistance to threat 84, 85
reducing gap between identity claims
and reputation 90d
reputation and identity conflict in
management consulting 88–90
sector level threats, example of 87–8
triple bottom line 9, 77d, 78

United Nations (UN) 143
bluewashing 49
Conference of the Parties (COP) 10,
73, 79
CSR, emphasis on 81
SDGs see Sustainable Development
Goals (SDGs)

values see purpose and values
virtual world 1, 6, 12, 74, 112, 145